PRAISE FOR
SEX, LIES AND THE BALLOT BOX

Sex, Lies and the Ballot Box takes you inside the darkest recesses of the voter's mind – and bedroom.

It asks why we vote the way we do, why we make stuff up when we're asked and whether we are even conscious of the forces that inform our choices.

If you love elections you'll be hooked from page one. If you never vote but want to know how your sex life reflects your politics, then start at the end and work backwards. Either way – it's a complete riot. Smart, funny and illuminating in ways you could never dream of.

— **EMILY MAITLIS**

This book is such an utterly brilliant idea it is ridiculous that no one has thought of it before.

Ask fifty specialists in their field to write very short chapters summarising an area of research as if they were explaining it to an intelligent non-specialist, emphasising the bizarre, or at least unexpected, human psychology revealed by their findings.

The result is a surprising amount of sex and quite a lot of human frailty. This is how academics ought to relate to people. This is a wonderfully readable book. You can dip in and out of it, and every trip into its pages will be longer than you intended, and you will emerge miraculously better informed. I cannot recommend it highly enough.

— **JOHN RENTOUL**

SEX, LIES
& THE BALLOT BOX

SEX, LIES'

& THE BALLOT BOX

50 THINGS YOU NEED TO KNOW ABOUT BRITISH ELECTIONS

EDITED BY

PHILIP COWLEY & ROBERT FORD

FOREWORD BY

DANIEL FINKELSTEIN

Biteback Publishing

First published in Great Britain in 2014 by
Biteback Publishing Ltd
Westminster Tower
3 Albert Embankment
London SE1 7SP

ISBN 978-1-84954-755-0

10 9 8 7 6 5 4 3 2 1

A CIP catalogue record for this book is available from the British Library.

Set in Minion Pro

Printed and bound in Great Britain by
CPI Group (UK) Ltd, Croydon CR0 4YY

To David Butler, on his ninetieth birthday

Contents

Foreword

Daniel Finkelstein

Is there any point to this? Why are we bothering?

There can't be anyone who has gone canvassing and hasn't wondered this at least once – especially when no one answers the door. One evening I expressed surprise at how many people called Friedland there seemed to be in the constituency, and all of them out. This was how I first learned that Friedland made doorbells.

The feeling is quickly suppressed, of course, and for all sorts of sloppy reasons. If you don't suppress the feeling then it is hard to carry on. And you are expected to carry on: it is a social necessity within parties, and a political one if you want to be a candidate. Anyway, you know a couple of people who did a lot of work and won, plus don't the Liberal Democrats do it? You have to do something, and this is something, so you'd better do it.

Yet this sloppy reasoning is unnecessary. 'Is there any point to this?' is a testable proposition. Using either field experiments or, potentially, identifying large data sets and surveys, it would be possible to establish reasonably conclusively whether canvassing makes any difference.

Political scientists have known this for decades, of course – it's true of this, and it's true of many, many questions about political activity – yet the thought has only just begun to dawn among politicians and political commentators.

It has been routine, for instance, to comment on the budget's political impact, or that of a leader's conference speech, without considering all the studies that either have been done or could be done, on how people absorb political messages and the difference those messages make to voting behaviour.

During the recent American presidential election, for instance, I was quite shocked by the extent to which sophisticated analysts relied on hunch and hopes rather than on the copious amount of research that could, and should, have informed their judgements.

Politicians and political commentators should accept the greatest amount of the blame for the gap between what we know and what we should know. But a little bit of the blame should go to political scientists too. They have sometimes spoken just to each other and in a way too obscure for the general reader to understand.

I think we are seeing a revolution in understanding now, and this book is part of it. Political scientists are making a huge effort to be seen and comprehended. They are forcing their data and conclusions on those who shouldn't be allowed simply to ignore them. At the same time, commentators are just beginning to appreciate the resource that is available to them.

To have asked researchers to make sharp, quick, accessible summaries of their work is a brilliant idea, and the authors in this book have done as they were asked. The essays are crisp and revealing and often counter-intuitive.

There is even an answer to the question 'Is there any point to this?' I won't spoil it for you.

Introduction

Philip Cowley and Robert Ford

There are, apparently, people who don't find elections interesting. It's not a view we understand or have ever shared. For as long as either of us can remember, we've found elections – and all of the hoopla that goes along with them – fascinating. You may well be someone like us: the sort of person who stays up into the small hours to watch election results come in or who can quote opinion poll figures from memory. If you are, then we hope you enjoy this book. It is written *by* people like you, and, at least in part, it is written *for* people like you.

But it is also written for another audience: those who don't currently share our passion, and who might even think elections are a bit dull. If you are one of these people, then the book is also written for you, in the hope that we can change your mind.* People sometimes try to justify the study of elections and voting on the basis that they are an important part of democracy. True, but things can be important without being interesting. Elections are both important *and* interesting. The fundamental reason elections are interesting is because they involve people: those who stand; those who vote for them; those who

---

* The tricky thing, presumably, will be to get you reading it in the first place, given your attitude, but perhaps you've been lured in by the reference to sex, or perhaps you've been given it as an unwanted birthday present, or perhaps (hopefully, maybe?) someone's recommended it. Either way, stick with us.

don't vote at all. Like most things involving people, explaining what they do and why they do it is not always straightforward. Sometimes it is depressing, sometimes it is uplifting, but it is always revealing. Elections offer an insight into who we are and how we behave as good as you will get from any psychologist's couch.

It's not always a flattering insight. The ideal voter of traditional liberal thought is a rational man or woman, who gathers all the evidence about the issues of the day and the plans of the parties, weighs it all up responsibly, cogitating at length, and then delivers a mature and informed judgement at the ballot box. The reality of elections isn't much like this. Voters are influenced by emotion, by ignorance and by prejudice. They often have little awareness of what the parties are proposing and can be swayed by the most trivial or superficial matters. To take two examples from the following pages, these include how attractive the candidates are and the order in which they appear on the ballot paper (earlier is better, as reading all the way to the bottom takes effort).

All of this might cause headaches for liberal theorists of democracy; that's their problem. To us it just makes the electoral process even more interesting. But don't make the mistake – as some do – of thinking that voters are thick. One of the many titles considered but rejected for this volume was *The Stupid Voter*; we rejected it pretty swiftly, because even when voters are wrong, they're not stupid. By contrast, they can often be calculating. Even ignorance can be rational: many voters reason, correctly, that learning the details of policy is not worth the effort as it won't change their choice. And while some voters are wildly ill-informed and can make bizarre choices, this individual-level eccentricity tends to cancel out. In the aggregate, as a mass, voters are often rational and responsive. There is wisdom in crowds, something politicians ignore at their peril.

In electoral terms, we have – to quote Harold Macmillan – never had it so good. For one thing, there are just more of them than there used to be. In addition to Westminster and local elections, we now have devolved elections in Scotland, Wales and Northern Ireland, along with elections for the European Parliament and a scattering of mayoral contests. We even think the elections for Police and Crime Commissioners in England and Wales are interesting, although judging from the turnout we may be the only ones. Almost every year now brings some significant electoral battle. These various elections use a variety of different electoral systems. Plus we make more use of referendums than we used to, providing another insight into public opinion. Whatever your views on the outcome of the Scottish independence referendum, anyone who didn't find the campaign interesting just wasn't paying attention. This transformation of the UK into an electoral laboratory has been great news for psephologists, if not always for voters.

As Lyndon Johnson observed, the first lesson of politics is to be able to count. One of the great problems with much past coverage of politics is that it was written and read by people who had not learned LBJ's lesson. The opening book in the 'Nuffield' election series – *The British General Election of 1945* – gives a long list of 'named' elections: 1874, when the Liberals went down in a flood of gin and beer; the Midlothian election of 1880; the khaki election of 1900; the Chinese Slavery election of 1906; the People's Budget election of 1910; the 'Hang the Kaiser' election of 1918; and the 1924 'Zinoviev letter' election. People named these elections after high profile factors which featured heavily in the campaigns, and which then became the consensus explanation for the outcome. The great human urge for story telling often leads us astray when it comes to elections: the magnificent complexity and contradiction of a collective decision made by millions is reduced to a single issue or campaign argument.

Things have changed since the Nuffield studies began. Nowadays, more of the many things which matter in politics are counted, more of those following politics can count and more of them have better tools to help do the sums. We can now measure the work the parties do in their central offices and their constituency branches; we can track the ebb and flow of public opinion with greater precision and weigh it against the myriad economic and social forces which influence voters' judgements. Many of the chapters in this book, for example, draw on data from the comprehensive British Election Study, which has now been running continuously since the election of 1964, making it the longest-running electoral study in Europe and allowing us to quantify and analyse the ups and downs of mass politics over a sweep of fifty years. There are now also far more 'normal' opinion polls than ever before, as the arrival of internet polling has massively pushed down the costs of data collection. This allows the commissioning of research that would not have been pragmatically possible before. Several of the chapters in this volume draw on experiments conducted with thousands of survey respondents. In the days of polling using clipboard and pencil, such an undertaking would have been unthinkable.

We no longer give elections single names because, armed with this wealth of data, we now know it is absurd to imagine that a single issue or controversy could have the power to decide the outcome. The siren call of storytelling still has the power to lead people astray, however. The 2005 election is sometimes still discussed as the 'Iraq election', reflecting the extent to which elite debate focused on the consequences and justifications of the 2003 war. But we know that, for most voters, Iraq came relatively low down the list of concerns. A generation earlier, Margaret Thatcher's first re-election was deemed by some to be the result of the 'Falklands Factor', but there is also plenty of evidence showing that the Falklands War was much less significant than people thought at the time. As we write, many are singling out Ed Miliband's weakness with the electorate, Conservative divides over the EU or Nick Clegg's precipitous decline in the eyes of voters as *the* factor which will decide next year's election. Those who have taken LBJ's lesson to heart will know that the true story of 2015 – like all the previous elections – will be far more complicated and far more interesting than that.

No one who does it seriously thinks that measuring public opinion is without difficulties. Several of the chapters in this volume highlight some of the problems: different responses to almost identical questions; inconsistent attitudes; voters who support or oppose policies that do not exist; voters who think they voted when they didn't (and think they didn't when they did). There is an exchange in *Yes, Minister* between Humphrey and Bernard, after Bernard presents some unwelcome opinion poll data and is told to go away and do another poll producing the opposite response. Bernard protests that the public can't be both for and against something. Sir Humphrey's response: 'Of course they can, Bernard.' And Sir Humphrey was right. But, however tricky, attempting to measure public opinion is still better than the alternative, which is not to measure it at all and just assume you know it based on what you and those around you think.

In the run-up to the 2005 election, one of us was phoned up by a journalist from the *New Statesman* who wondered how the polls could possibly be showing a Labour lead, given that no one in their office was intending to vote Labour. This said more about the *New Statesman* than it did about the British public. None of us are blessed with friends and acquaintances that form a representative sample of the British public and we're all prone to think that our views are somehow typical and normal. A good example from the following chapters is the tenth anniversary of the Iraq War when a spate of newspaper articles were produced – often written by twenty-somethings who had been on anti-war marches in their teens – claiming that the war had turned most young people off politics. This might be true for the writers and their peers. Yet, as one of the chapters in this book shows, they were no more representative of public opinion generally than the *New Statesman* staff. Young people are no more or less involved in politics now than they were before the Iraq War.

Another example of a common misconception, also from the following chapters, is that money determines British elections. Yet, as one of our contributors shows, there's very little evidence to suggest it makes much of a difference. Another example is that elections are now fought and won on TV. Yet, as later chapters show, the grassroots campaign still matters and can often be decisive. If the parties knock on your door, it's because they (unlike some media commentators) know it might make a difference. And if they don't knock on your door, it's because they are struggling to recruit people to do so – or because there are fewer marginal seats than before and you are unlucky (or lucky, depending on how you look at it) to live in a constituency that isn't likely to change hands.

Knowing more about voters does not make it easier to predict what they will do. In fact, the opposite is true of British voters. We may know more about them, but one of the things that this has revealed is that they are becoming much more unpredictable. This highlights a real problem with golden ageism when discussing British elections. Yes, voters were more satisfied with politics and turned out in elections more in the '50s, but they were often locked into tribal partisan allegiances, voting the way they did out of habit and knowing very little about the policies or parties they supported. This isn't to say that today's voter is all-knowing and wise – as will become clear in the rest of this book – but they are now more volatile, demanding and changeable. This makes life harder for political parties, who can no longer rely on herding their traditional voters to the polling booth, but it makes voters much more interesting to study and, perhaps, makes our democracy more responsive and accountable to boot.

A word on the (eventual) title: we give you lies (those some voters tell over whether they voted and the ways they fib to opinion pollsters about their views on political issues); we give you sex (both in the sense of gender, but also in the sense of the bedroom); and we give you plenty of ballot box. Our authors look at: the process of getting people to the ballot box; how and why they then vote; the way their votes are then translated into seats; and what happens to those who stand for their parties and to those who lead them.

This is not – absolutely, categorically not – an introductory textbook. There are plenty of these on the market; indeed, several of the contributors to this volume have written such books, so we'd get into trouble if we recommended any one of them. This is not a compendium or an atlas, but a series of thumbnail sketches, each introducing an aspect of elections and electoral behaviour. In what follows, we don't claim to cover every topic, but the following fifty chapters incorporate: polling, political geography, gender, sex, race, grassroots campaigning, money, Scotland, candidates, electoral bias, tactical voting, the old media, the new media, leaders, the economy, Wales, tactical voting, young people, prejudice, money, knowledge, rationality, emotions, social pressure, Northern Ireland, attractiveness, party members, candidates, group norms, exit polls, and class. Plus cats. Just in case that's not enough, there's a bonus fifty-first chapter giving you even more sex.

Among the many thing covered in the following pages, our contributors explain why 35 per cent of the popular vote can give you a comfortable 66-seat majority in the House of Commons, but 36 per cent of the vote can also leave you twenty seats short of a majority.

They identify the most left-wing (Glasgow North East) and right-wing (Surrey Heath) constituencies in Britain.

They show how one party is both the biggest winner and the biggest loser from tactical voting.

They show the huge political importance of those you live with. Live in a house in which one person votes and you're 90 per cent certain to vote yourself. Live with a non-voter and that figure falls to less than 10 per cent.

They show mums really do know best: they are a much bigger influence on the voting of their children than fathers.

They show how emotions matter and leaders matter (although not always as you might think) and how partisanship colours your views of everything, even pets.

They show that class matters less than it used to, gender doesn't matter very much, but ethnicity matters a great deal. Why do ethnic minorities overwhelmingly vote Labour? It's not because they share Labour's values.

They show how party image extends even into the bedroom. The public have very different views of how a Labour supporter will behave between the sheets compared to a Conservative and, even more astonishingly, they show how some of these differences really do exist. Conservatives and Labour supporters do report very different sex lives and this isn't just because different types of people support different parties; these partisan effects remain even after we take that into account. If you want to know which type of party supporter is most likely to use a vibrator (and to fantasise about vibrators), read on.

The chapters are written by members of the Political Studies Association's specialist group on Elections, Public Opinion and Parties, known as EPOP, which has been running for over twenty years. It is a vibrant and productive group, one of the PSA's most active. We're happy to report that, despite the many demands of academic life, colleagues were extremely enthusiastic about the project when we pitched it to them. In most cases, the underpinning work reported here is much more complicated, but we have explicitly asked authors to present it in as accessible a way as possible. If you find yourself thinking 'very interesting, but did they consider X', the answer is almost certainly yes (and they probably considered Y and Z as well). These are 1,000-word essays, not monographs, each summarising years, in some cases decades, of research. Each chapter ends with a short account of further reading and there is a detailed bibliography in case any of the subject matter stirs you to dig deeper.

Anyone who's ever dealt with academics will understand that coordinating fifty or so of them wasn't always easy, but we're grateful to all of them for their enthusiasm for the project (undimmed by repeated editorial requests) and the quality of their contributions. We are also grateful to all the staff at Biteback for their fantastic support. We hope you think the end result is worth it.

List of contributors

TIM BALE is Professor of Politics at Queen Mary, University of London.

GALINA BORISYUK is Lecturer in Advanced Quantitative Research Methods in Political Science at Plymouth University.

ROSIE CAMPBELL is Reader in Politics at Birkbeck, University of London.

MARTA CANTIJOCH is Q-Step Lecturer in Politics at the University of Manchester.

ALISTAIR CLARK is Senior Lecturer in Politics at Newcastle University.

HAROLD CLARKE is Ashbel Smith Professor in the School of Economic, Political and Policy Sciences at the University of Texas, Dallas.

PHILIP COWLEY is Professor of Parliamentary Government at the University of Nottingham.

JOHN CURTICE is Professor of Politics at Strathclyde University and Co-Director of the British and Scottish Social Attitudes Surveys.

DAVID CUTTS is Reader in Political Science at the University of Bath.

DAVID DENVER is Emeritus Professor of Politics at Lancaster University.

DANNY DORLING is Halford Mackinder Professor of Geography at the University of Oxford.

CEES VAN DER EIJK is Professor of Social Science Research Methods and Director of Social Sciences Methods and Data Institute at the University of Nottingham.

ELIZABETH EVANS is Lecturer in Politics at the University of Bristol.

GEOFF EVANS is Official Fellow in Politics at Nuffield College, Oxford, and Professor of the Sociology of Politics at the University of Oxford.

JOCELYN EVANS is Professor of Politics at the University of Leeds.

JUSTIN FISHER is Professor of Political Science and Director of the Magna Carta Institute at Brunel University.

STEPHEN FISHER is the Fellow and Tutor in Politics at Trinity College, Oxford, and Associate Professor in Political Sociology at the University of Oxford.

ROBERT FORD is Senior Lecturer in Politics at the University of Manchester.

STUART FOX is a PhD student at the University of Nottingham.

MATTHEW GOODWIN is Associate Professor of Politics at the University of Nottingham.

CHRIS HANRETTY is Reader in Politics at the University of East Anglia.

ANTHONY HEATH is Emeritus Professor of Sociology at the University of Oxford and the University of Manchester and Emeritus Fellow of Nuffield College, Oxford, where he is Director of the Centre for Social Investigation.

JENNIFER VAN HEERDE-HUDSON is Senior Lecturer in Political Behaviour at University College London.

AILSA HENDERSON is Professor of Political Science and Head of Politics and International Relations at the University of Edinburgh.

WILL JENNINGS is Professor of Political Science and Public Policy at the University of Southampton.

ROB JOHNS is Senior Lecturer in Politics at the University of Essex.

RON JOHNSTON is Professor of Geography at the University of Bristol.

CAITLIN MILAZZO is Assistant Professor in Politics at the University of Nottingham.

ALISON PARK is Director of Society and Social Change at NatCen Social Research.

CHARLES PATTIE is Professor of Geography at the University of Sheffield.

COLIN RALLINGS is Professor of Politics at Plymouth University.

ALAN RENWICK is Associate Professor in Comparative Politics at the University of Reading.

ELINE DE ROOIJ did her DPhil at Nuffield College, Oxford, and is Assistant Professor at Simon Fraser University.

GEMMA ROSENBLATT is research strategy manager at the Electoral Commission.

DAVID ROSSITER is a retired Research Fellow who formerly worked at the Universities of Bristol, Leeds, Oxford and Sheffield.

ANDREW RUSSELL is Professor of Politics at the University of Manchester.

DAVID SANDERS is Regius Professor of Political Science at the University of Essex.

ROGER SCULLY is Professor of Political Science in the Wales Governance Centre at Cardiff University.

MARIA SOBOLEWSKA is Lecturer in Politics (Quantitative Methods) at the University of Manchester.

DANIEL STEVENS is Associate Professor at the University of Exeter.

PATRICK STURGIS is Professor of Research Methodology and Director of the National Centre for Research Methods at the University of Southampton.

MICHAEL THRASHER is Professor of Politics and Director of the Elections Centre at Plymouth University.

JAMES TILLEY is a Fellow of Jesus College, Oxford, and University Lecturer in the Department of Politics and International Relations at the University of Oxford.

JON TONGE is Professor of Politics at the University of Liverpool.

JOE TWYMAN is Head of Political and Social Research (Europe, Middle East and Africa) at YouGov.

NICK VIVYAN is Lecturer in Quantitative Social Research at Durham University.

MARKUS WAGNER is Assistant Professor in quantitative methods at the University of Vienna.

ANTHONY WELLS is Associate Director of YouGov's political polling team and writes the independent UKPollingReport.co.uk blog.

PAUL WHITELEY is Professor of Politics at the University of Essex.

BERNADETA WILK is Associate Director within the Analytics Team at YouGov.

KRISTI WINTERS conducted the 2010 Qualitative Election Study of Britain.

'The people have spoken, the bastards.'

DICK TUCK, AFTER LOSING A CALIFORNIA STATE SENATE RACE IN 1966

—CHAPTER 1—

Slippery polls:
why public opinion
is so difficult to measure

Rob Johns

Imagine a fantasy world in which the British government wanted only to follow public opinion. With no agenda of its own, the Cabinet would sit down weekly to plan how to translate the latest polls directly into public policy. This government would find life very difficult; it would be prone to frequent U-turns and would rapidly become frustrated with its public masters. The problem is the slippery nature of opinion polls. Questions asked about the same issue on the same day can often carry different, even directly contradictory, messages about public preferences.

One common explanation for this, the case of deliberately leading questions, can be swiftly dismissed. Everyone knows that a question along the lines of 'do you support Policy X or do you oppose this ill-conceived and dangerous idea?' will reduce support for Policy X, and the major pollsters refuse to field such obviously biased questions. Such blatant bias is now largely confined to opt-in polls on tabloid newspaper websites.

The real difficulty for pollsters and those poring over their results is that even ostensibly neutral questions can be strikingly inconsistent. Consider one of the earliest question-wording experiments, a 1940 survey in which American respondents were randomly chosen to receive one of two questions about free speech. The results are in the table, which also shows what happened when the experiment was re-run three decades later. Americans in 1940 were a lot more comfortable in 'not allowing' (75 per cent) than in 'forbidding' (54 per cent) speeches against democracy. By 1974, the results were more befitting of the Land of the Free but the big difference between question wordings remained. The nature of that difference makes sense – forbidding something sounds harsher than merely not allowing it – but its scale is troubling. Are public preferences on issues as fundamental as free speech really so weak as to be dramatically shifted by a change in emphasis?

THE FORBID/ALLOW ASYMMETRY IN QUESTION-WORDING

	ALLOW/ NOT FORBID (%)	NOT ALLOW/ FORBID (%)
1940 EXPERIMENT		
Group A: Do you think the US should allow public speeches against democracy?	25	75
Group B: Do you think the US should forbid public speeches against democracy?	46	54
1974 EXPERIMENT		
Group A: Allow public speeches against democracy?	52	48
Group B: Forbid public speeches against democracy?	71	21

To answer that question, it is useful to sketch Paul (or Paula), the typical survey respondent. Politics is low on his agenda and, as a result, many of the questions asked by pollsters are on issues to which Paul has given little previous thought. As American researcher Philip

Converse concluded, many people simply 'do not have meaningful beliefs, even on issues that have formed the basis for intense political controversy among elites for substantial periods of time'. But Paul is an obliging type and can't help feeling that, if a pollster is asking him about an issue, he really ought to have a view on it. So he will avoid saying 'don't know' and oblige with an answer. (As Chapter 2 shows, respondents are often happy to answer even when pollsters ask about fictional policies.)

How, then, does Paul answer these questions? Not purely at random because, even with unfamiliar issues, there are links to more familiar and deeply held attitudes and values. For example, if Paul were asked about British military intervention in Syria, he might support action on humanitarian grounds or oppose action on the pragmatic basis that other recent interventions were not an unalloyed success. None of this requires Paul even to know where Syria is on the map. However, the other thing about Paul is that he is a little lazy, at least in cognitive terms. Rather than addressing the question from all relevant angles, balancing conflicting considerations to reach a judgement, he is prone to answer on the basis of whatever comes immediately to mind. If the previous night's news contained graphic images of humanitarian crisis, Paul will probably support intervention; if instead there was a story about defence spending cuts, he is likely to oppose it. This 'top-of-the-head' nature of survey answers is what gives the question wording such power. Any small cue or steer in the question is, by definition, at the top of people's heads when answering.

Attributions are one common cue. In the early 2000s the Conservative Party found that many of its new ideas were quite popular in opinion polls – unless the poll mentioned that they were Conservative policies, in which case that popularity ebbed. If a policy of intervention in Syria was attributed to David Cameron or his government, respondents might just respond according to their partisan sympathies (see Chapter 4 for how this applies even to cats).

Now imagine that the question about Syrian intervention ended with 'even if this involved substantial British military casualties'. Paul and many others would be far less likely to support action. This doesn't mean military casualties are *really* a decisive factor in public judgements; it means that the question elbows other considerations out of respondents' minds. Or suppose that the Syrian intervention question itself was studiedly neutral but that it was preceded by a series of questions about British casualties in Iraq and Afghanistan. The effect would be much the same.

Another common steer comes in those questions based on declarative statements. For example, another survey experiment found majority agreement (60 per cent) with the statement: 'Individuals are more to blame than social conditions for crime in this country.' But the survey also found almost the same level of agreement (57 per cent) with the exact opposite statement: 'Social conditions are more to blame than individuals for crime in this country.' This is because the statements used in the question have persuasive power in themselves. It is easier for unsure (and lazy) respondents to agree with the assertion than consider the alternatives.

Along similar lines, consider the Scottish government's original proposal for the 2014 referendum question: 'Do you agree that Scotland should be an independent country?' Or the GCSE Statistics paper which asked students to explain why the question 'Do you agree that canteen food is value for money?' is biased. In both cases the words 'or disagree' should be inserted to induce obliging-but-lazy respondents at least to consider that alternative.

Lastly, consider the choice between open and closed questions. Polls often ask 'What do you think is the most important problem facing Britain today?' In the 'closed' version, where respondents choose from a list, crime is a popular choice. Yet in an 'open' version, where respondents have to name an issue unprompted, crime is much less often mentioned. Maybe a list helps to remind people of their genuine concerns, but then is crime *that* troubling to someone who can't remember it unaided?

All of this illustrates the persistent difficulty for our fantasy government. Even the most discerning consumer of opinion polls, who well understands why two surveys deliver different results, might still struggle to say which better reflects what the public really thinks. Some have even drawn the radical conclusion that 'true' attitudes simply don't exist. This seems overstated, however. For one thing, people do have strong views on the big issues that they care about. It is when pollsters ask about more remote topics that opinions look so fickle. Second, even when respondents appear malleable, this is not simply swaying in the breeze; it is because something in the question leads them to consider the issue in a different way.

Public opinion thus has at least some anchoring in people's most deeply held beliefs and values. Perhaps a preferable conclusion is that the truths are out there – but that there are many of them and they may be quite different. This, of course, provides exactly the leeway that real governments are after.

FURTHER READING

The quotation from Philip Converse is taken from his 1964 essay on 'The nature of belief systems in mass publics'. A 'one-stop shop' for question-wording effects is the book *Questions and Answers in Attitude Surveys* by Howard Schuman and Stanley Presser (Sage, 1996). For informed commentary on UK opinion polling, with frequent reminders of the pitfalls discussed in this chapter, consult Anthony Wells's blog UK Polling Report.

— CHAPTER 2 —

Why one in ten Britons support the Monetary Control Bill (even though it doesn't exist): public opinion and nonattitudes

Patrick Sturgis

In nearly every survey there are some people who tell pollsters that they do not have an opinion on an issue. But the number willing to volunteer ignorance in this way often appears rather smaller than it should be, given that many people know and care very little about politics. How, then, do voters decide where they stand on unfamiliar areas of public policy when asked about them in polls?

As noted in Chapter 1, a radical answer to this question was proposed in the '60s by American political scientist, Philip Converse. Converse suggested that, on many issues, a substantial minority of the public has no opinion at all. Rather, they express what he referred to as 'nonattitudes'. A nonattitude is an answer to an opinion question which has no underlying cognitive or emotional basis; people select from the available response options more or less at random, as if 'mentally flipping a coin'.

If true, the implications for democratic politics, as well as for the polling industry, would be problematic.

It is difficult to assess how big a problem nonattitudes really are, however, because from their outwardly observable characteristics at least, attitudes and nonattitudes are identical. An expedient solution to the problem of identifying the prevalence of nonattitudes is to ask people their opinions on issues which sound real but do not actually exist. People who are willing to provide an opinion on a plausible-sounding but fictitious policy issue are, we may assume, also likely to offer similarly empty opinions on real issues which they know little or nothing about.

The idea of identifying nonattitudes in this way stretches back at least as far as the '40s, when pollster Sam Gill speculated that up to 70 per cent of Americans would provide an opinion on the (non-existent) Metallic Metals Act. However, serious academic consideration of public opinion about fictitious issues did not start until the '80s, when George Bishop and colleagues at the University of Cincinnati found that a third of Americans either favoured or opposed the fictitious Public Affairs Act. Bishop found that this figure dropped substantially when respondents were offered an explicit 'don't know' option. However, 10 per cent of respondents still selected a substantive answer, even when given a clear opportunity to express their lack of familiarity. Similar findings were reported in the US at around the same time by Howard Schuman and Stanley Presser, who also found that a third of respondents to their survey expressed positions on issues which, though real, were so obscure that few ordinary citizens would ever have heard of them.

And, despite the British generally considering themselves to be intellectually superior to their American cousins, recent research found significant proportions of the British public were also willing to express views on fictitious policy issues. It isn't possible to make direct comparisons between the British and the American research, because the questions posed and response alternatives offered were rather different. However, the British study found that 15 per cent of the British public either supported or opposed the non-existent 'Monetary Control Bill', while 11 per cent expressed a position on the equally fictitious 'Agricultural Trade Bill'.

So, non-trivial numbers of citizens are willing to offer opinions on issues which do not exist. Are they really selecting a response option at random as Converse suggested? Probably not. Research has shown that responses to these fictitious issues are related to existing partisan tendencies. For example, in the British research, Conservative supporters were twice as likely to express an opinion on the Agricultural Trade Bill, compared to people who did not identify with a political party. This suggests that respondents do not choose their answers to fictitious issues at random but, rather, seek to determine what the issue is about and how it relates to their political predispositions, through clues in the wording of the question. In this instance, 'agricultural trade' sounds like legislation promoting free trade, so Conservative supporters interpret it as something which they should, on the face of it at least, favour.

Another sign that these opinions are not just random expressions of ignorance comes from the somewhat counter-intuitive finding that people who reported being very interested in politics were more likely (23 per cent) to provide an opinion on the fictitious bills than those who expressed no interest at all (11 per cent). The British research also found that men were 50 per cent more likely to express a view on the Agricultural Trade Bill than women. So, responding to fictitious issues seems to result, at least in part, from considering yourself to be the sort of person who *should* have a view on matters of public interest. Many voters know little or nothing about more obscure parts of the political agenda but voters who initially proclaim their general interest in politics may be too embarrassed to admit ignorance when subsequently asked their position on specific issues.

Despite the seemingly flippant nature of the exercise, then, research on fictitious issues tells us at least two interesting things about how people respond to questions relating to real policy issues in polls and surveys. First, people do not choose a response option at random from the tops of their heads but are, instead, actively seeking to understand what the question is about. They then provide their best guess at what their position is, based on their political orientation and the limited information available to them about the issue. This helps explain why the 'framing' of a survey question can matter so much to the shape of public opinion elicited; the exact terms used to describe an issue can strongly affect how voters understand what it is about and, therefore, how they feel about it. Be that as it may, fictitious issues research also tells us that a great many answers to genuine policy questions in surveys are likely to be based on little more than informed guessing, following a brief moment of reflection. This may not come as a surprise to many observers of contemporary politics. However, it serves as a cautionary reminder to all those who proffer opinion poll evidence in order to show they have public backing for a particular policy position; the mandate they are citing is probably weaker than it appears.

FURTHER READING

Bishop's study on the US is 'Pseudo-Opinions on Public Affairs' by George Bishop et al. (*Public Opinion Quarterly*, 1980). The British study can be found in Patrick Sturgis and Patten Smith 'Fictitious Issues Revisited: Political Interest, Knowledge and the Generation of Nonattitudes' (*Political Studies*, 2010). Other relevant studies are Howard Schuman and Stanley Presser's 'Public Opinion and Public Ignorance: The Fine Line between Attitudes and Nonattitudes' (*American Journal of Sociology*, 1980) and George Bishop's *The Illusion of Public Opinion: Fact and Artifact in American Public Opinion Polls* (Rowman & Littlefield, 2005).

CHAPTER 3

Why the next election will not be decided by gay marriage: meaningless polling questions

Anthony Wells

Every scandal and surprise in politics inevitably prompts a debate over what it means for the parties' standings. The most sensible (but dull) way of testing this is to compare voting intentions before and after the event to see if there has been any effect. The alternative approach is to ask people directly if the event has changed how they will vote. In a perfect world these two approaches would show the same result. In practice they often don't.

In *The Independent* in January 2013 a ComRes poll found 30 per cent of people agreeing they were more likely to vote Conservative because David Cameron had promised to hold a referendum on Europe. In the month leading up to Cameron's pledge the average level of Conservative support in the polls was 31 per cent. In the month following, the average was still 31 per cent. Despite the poll, the pledge had made no difference.

Europe is unlikely to change many voters' minds at any time: it is an issue that greatly excites Conservative backbench MPs, but few others; even the growth of support for UKIP in recent years owes more to the issue of immigration than to Europe. But this still leaves the mystery of why so many would *claim* that the issue had the power to change their minds, when it clearly does not.

One reason is that such questions take an issue out of context and give it false prominence. If you only ask questions about, say, transport then people responding to your poll will think it is something important that they *should* care about. However come the election the issue will take its place in the public debate alongside issues like the economy, the NHS, or pensions and soon fade to insignificance.

Second, respondents to surveys are not lab rats. You can't blind people to the fact they are taking part in a survey, and people can and will use the question to indicate their support or opposition to a policy, regardless of whether it really would change their vote. 'This would change my vote' is really, for many, a way of saying 'I have an opinion about this'.

The third problem is that people tend to report the answers to such questions in a way that neglects the current party support of those who responded. If you ask a question about whether a policy would make people more or less likely to vote Tory then you'll often find that the majority of people who say the policy would make them more likely to vote Tory are already staunch Conservatives, while the majority of people who say it would make them less likely to vote Tory are people who would never vote Tory anyway. And 'more likely' isn't a very high bar; if a policy proposal has changed someone's likelihood of voting Conservative from 95 per cent to 99 per cent then it has made little substantive difference.

People are also poor judges of what drives their own voting intentions. As many chapters in this book demonstrate, in politics, as in many other areas of life, we do not actually understand our own decision-making processes very well; our decisions are based far more upon our own prejudices, biases and tribal attachments than we would like to imagine.

Despite all these problems, these types of questions are sadly irresistible to journalists. For example, in 2009 44 per cent of people said they'd be much less likely to vote for a party that disconnected the internet for people who shared pirated software; in 2013 22 per cent of people said they would be less likely to vote Labour if Labour members of the House of Lords blocked the passage of the Referendum Bill. In the same year, another poll found 26 per cent of people would be less likely to vote Tory if they made it easier for farmers to shoot foxes for pest control. The silliness of questions like this should be immediately clear: the idea that *several million* people might change their vote because of punishments for file-sharers or rules on when farmers can shoot foxes is patently absurd.

Polls like this reached a nadir with the debate over gay marriage in 2013. For months newspapers treated us to reports claiming that 'Gay marriage could cost Conservatives power', accompanied by poll findings apparently showing that same-sex marriage was costing the Conservatives large chunks of support. In April 2013 a poll in areas with local elections found 23 per cent of people said they were less likely to vote Tory in local elections because of gay marriage, including 26 per cent of people who voted Tory in 2010. (They included 12 per cent of the sample who said they would vote Conservative at the local elections – a case, one assumes, of 'Lord, make me less likely to vote Tory … but not just yet'.) Another poll in January 2013 found 20 per cent of 2010 Tories agreeing that 'I would have considered voting Conservative at the next election but will definitely not if the coalition government legalises same-sex marriage'.

Given the prominence of the debate, YouGov (for whom I work) tried to get round as many of the issues as possible. We hid gay marriage among a longer list of issues and asked people to pick those most likely to influence their vote, then asked those who did say same-sex marriage in which way it would influence them. That found only 7 per cent said that same-sex marriage was a subject that would influence their vote, and by 54 per cent to 44 per cent, that subset of voters said they were *more*, not less, likely to vote for a party that supported gay marriage. The majority of these respondents didn't vote Conservative in 2010 anyway, so these were not the 'lost Tory voters' the media were focusing on. Among 2010 Tory voters only 4 per cent said same-sex marriage would be an important factor in deciding their vote and that they would be less likely to vote for a party that supported it. That is, one in twenty-five, not one in four, showing that gay marriage was dwarfed by issues like the running of the economy and public services.

Even this isn't an especially *good* measure of the direct impact of gay marriage at the general election, but it's better than surveys chasing easy publicity. People will still be poor judges of their own motivations and focusing on issues alone still misses out major factors that we know drive voting intentions, such as leadership perceptions and party identification. Voting is too complicated to deal with in one question, and you should probably steer clear of any poll that claims to do so.

FURTHER READING

For a far more solid look at what drives voting intentions based on serious analysis of polling data, look to the work of the British Election Study, most recently *Affluence, Austerity and Electoral Change in Britain* by Paul Whiteley et al. (Cambridge University Press, 2013). While it predates the rise of internet polling, for a more general overview of British political opinion polling the best book remains Nick Moon's *Opinion Polls: History, Theory and Practice* (Manchester University Press, 1999).

—CHAPTER 4—

Of mousers and men: how politics colours everything we see

Robert Ford

One important staffing decision David Cameron took early in his premiership was to fill the post of Chief Mouser, which had been vacant since the demise of its previous occupant, Sybil, at the height of the global financial crisis. Defying their party's commitment to lean government, the Conservatives made two appointments: Larry and Freya. These cats are the latest in a long line of Downing Street felines, stretching back at least to Churchill's time in office. Incumbents often hold the role for a long time: Mrs Thatcher's cat, Humphrey (allegedly named after a fictional civil servant with similar feline cunning), remained in office through the rest of her term, and that of her successor John Major, finally retiring from service in 10 Downing Street during Tony Blair's first term in office.

Like all Whitehall civil servants, the Downing Street cats are resolutely apolitical, serving at the pleasure of Her Majesty's government, whichever political tribe takes the helm. But this is not how they are seen by the electorate. In an experiment run with the survey company YouGov, a representative sample of voters were shown a picture of the redoubtable Humphrey randomly varying whether he was described as Margaret Thatcher's cat or Tony Blair's cat and asked to say whether they liked or disliked him. The figure below shows how the net approval of Humphrey the cat (the share who like Humphrey minus the share who dislike him) varies depending on the partisanship of the respondents doing the rating, and the Prime Minister with whom Humphrey is associated.

NET APPROVAL OF HUMPHREY THE CAT BY PARTISANSHIP AND DESCRIPTION OF OWNER

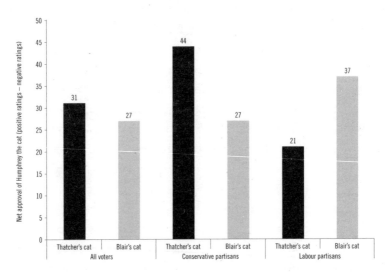

Source: YouGov poll of 2,190 voters, April 2014

Humphrey comes out with a strongly positive net rating (unlike most of the politicians he served) and his overall rating among all voters is not much affected by association with Thatcher or Blair. The views of partisan respondents, however, are strongly affected by Humphrey's perceived owner. Conservative voters show a much stronger affection for Mrs Thatcher's cat than for an identical cat associated with Mr Blair, while Labour partisans show the opposite preference. The same was true in a second experiment using pictures of the (different) cats resident in Downing Street during Gordon Brown and David Cameron's terms in office. Labour identifiers gave a cat associated with Gordon Brown a net rating of +50, but the same cat scored just +37 with Conservative partisans. Larry, Cameron's cat, scored +52 with Conservative identifiers but +40 with Labour loyalists. Nor is partisanship the only political attachment to influence views of the Chief Mouser: ideological values, views about national identity, gender and age are all associated with views of Humphrey and his successors, and these effects vary depending on the perceived owner. The public, it seems, buy into the theory that pets resemble their owners, but apply it to political outlook as well as appearance or personality.

The tale of Humphrey's politics illustrates a more serious point: our own political attachments and values tend to colour our views of anything and everything we associate with politics. Similar experiments conducted in the United States have shown that racially prejudiced Americans dislike Barack Obama's dog, which doesn't sound so harmful, but they also dislike any and every policy associated with Barack Obama, which certainly is. Racially intolerant Americans approved of Obama's reforms to expand access to health care for the young and the poor, but disapproved of identical reforms when they were associated with the President. One American late-night comedian confronted voters with this inconsistency, and found that many simply refused to believe that the health care reforms they supported were the same thing as the 'Obamacare' they rejected.

Attaching policies to politicians can thus short circuit entirely any rational consideration of their costs and benefits, replacing them with ideological and tribal loyalties. British researchers have found similar effects: voters interviewed around the time of the 1997 election tended to support policies associated with Tony Blair and Labour, but reject identical policies when they were attributed to John Major and the Conservatives, a phenomenon known as the 'halo and forked tail effect'. Partisanship also skews how voters judge responsibility: partisans are eager to give their preferred party credit for successes, and to absolve them from blame for failures.

In an idealised democracy, voters will assess the merits of policies and politicians, and then choose between them. In reality, voters often do the opposite: attached to one political tribe, their views of policies, politicians (and pets) are driven by whether these are seen as on our team or their team.

We should not be too harsh on the electorate. Politics is a complicated business, and voters are busy people. When they are presented with a difficult new problem they haven't considered before and know little about, such as education reform or banking regulation, they will naturally search for a shortcut. If the party they trust and support backs a reform, they will reason, it is probably a good idea. If the party they oppose and dislike is keen, then perhaps it is not. People use such intellectual shortcuts, known as heuristics, all the time: much of advertising is designed to exploit them. In a complicated and fast-moving world, it is hard to see how many of us could function without some shortcuts to reduce the torrent of information we face to more manageable proportions.

Yet a necessary survival strategy for voters – lean on what you do know when deciding about things you don't – poses troubling questions for the operation of a political system. How can new policies turn around the fortunes of an unpopular party, if even popular ideas become tainted by association? Should parties spend less time designing good policy, and more time building their brands and finding popular leaders? How much attention should politicians pay to the views of media and interest group elites, when such people spend most of their waking hours focused on politics, and therefore have little in common with the average voter, who rarely thinks about it at all? The next time you see a politician struggling to explain his latest ideas for solving the nation's problems, bear in mind that most of those watching are not going to give him a fair hearing including, most likely, you.

FURTHER READING

The experiment on Barack Obama's pet dog is described in Michael Tesler's 'The Spillover of Racialization into Evaluations of Bo Obama'. The broader range of experiments examining how support for policies is influenced by their association with Obama can be found in Tesler's 'The Spillover of Racialization into Health Care: How President Obama Polarized Public Opinion by Racial Attitudes and Race' (*American Journal of Political Science*, 2012) and *Obama's Race: The 2008 Election and the Dream of a Post-Racial America* by Tesler and David Sears (University of Chicago Press, 2010). The 'halo' and 'forked tail' effects found in the run-up to the 1997 British general election are described in *The Rise of New Labour: Party Policies and Voter Choices* by Anthony Heath et al. (Oxford University Press, 2001). The experiments demonstrating that partisanship determines how voters attribute credit and blame are found in James Tilley and Sara Hobolt's 'Is the Government to Blame? An Experimental Test of How Partisanship Shapes Perceptions of Performance and Responsibility' (*Journal of Politics*, 2011), but this does feature some daunting statistical material.

CHAPTER 5

Not total recall: why people lie about voting

Paul Whiteley

I t is quite a tricky problem to find out if people are telling the truth when they respond to surveys. One of the few opportunities to investigate this arises at election times, using the official records kept by local authorities to make sure that if an election is challenged they have a record of who actually voted. These records do not show *how* anyone voted, just whether they did, but they allow us to compare the reality with people's claims about what they did on polling day.

The 2010 British Election Study (BES) carried out checks on 3,515 respondents who took part in their survey. The following table compares claims of voting with actual voting for those survey respondents and it shows that there were significant numbers of people who gave misleading answers. The left-hand column in the table shows the respondent's validated vote obtained from the polling records after the election. The next two columns report the respondent's self-identified turnout in answer to a question in the post-election wave of the survey. Thus 55.6 per cent of all respondents claimed that they had voted in person when questioned in the survey, and the validation exercise confirmed that they did, indeed, vote. Similarly, 10.7 per cent of respondents said that they voted by post or by proxy and again the validation exercise reveals that they were telling the truth. Combining these two categories we find just over 66 per cent of people said they voted and did do so, which is approximately the same as the recorded turnout in the election.

REPORTED VOTE AND ACTUAL VOTING IN THE 2010 GENERAL ELECTION

VALIDATED VOTE	SELF-REPORTED VOTE		
	VOTED (%)	DID NOT VOTE (%)	TOTAL (%)
Voted in person	55.6	1.7	57.3
Postal/proxy vote	10.7	0.2	11.0
Not eligible to vote	0.3	0.4	0.7
Eligible but did not vote	6.3	13.6	19.9
Not on the register	5.0	6.2	11.2
TOTAL	**77.8**	**22.2**	**100.0**

Source: British Election Study 2010

The interesting section of the table relates to those who either did not remember what they did on election day or provided incorrect answers to the interviewer. Firstly, there are a number of respondents who said they voted but either could not, because they weren't on the electoral register, or did not, because the register confirmed they never cast a ballot. Some 5.3 per cent of all respondents claimed to have voted when they were actually ineligible or not on the register, and a further 6.3 per cent claimed to have voted, and were on the register, but never marked a ballot. Combining these categories, 11.6 per cent of survey respondents claimed to have participated in an election despite not doing so. At the time of the 2010 general election this represented about 5.3 million people so it is a significant group.

People also make mistakes in the opposite direction, claiming not to have voted when in fact they did: 1.7 per cent of respondents in the survey forgot that they had voted in person and a further 0.2 per cent forgot that they had voted by post or by proxy. But people are more likely to report false positives – that is, to have claimed to vote when they did not – than false negatives – forgetting that they have cast a ballot.

The standard explanation for this is that voting is seen as a desirable thing to do by most people, and so non-voters are tempted to claim that they have done it in order to conform to this social norm. Democracy is premised on the participation of the electorate, and many survey respondents are anxious to appear to be good citizens to an interviewer. However, plenty of people are happy to disregard this social norm: 13.6 per cent of interviewees declared truthfully that they did not vote, and another 6.2 per cent declared that they were non-voters who did not even feature on the electoral register. Add these groups together, and we find that one in five citizens is quite happy to ignore the social norm, sanctioning abstention. Young people are particularly likely to do this, since they have a weaker sense that voting is something expected of a good citizen. So while some of the over-reporting is likely to reflect a desire to conform to social norms, this is unlikely to tell the whole story.

One of the other questions in the BES survey in 2010 asked respondents about the likelihood of their voting in the general election. Responses were scored along an eleven-point scale where zero meant 'very unlikely' and ten meant 'very likely'. When this is analysed in comparison with records of voting, it turns out that high scores on this scale were associated with giving misleading answers to the question on turnout asked after the election. In other words, if individuals were unwilling to vote to begin with they were quite content to admit that they did not vote to an interviewer. But if they really wanted to vote and subsequently, for whatever reason, failed to do so, they were more likely to mislead the interviewers.

The psychologist Dan Ariely claims that behaviour like this is driven by two opposing motivations – what he calls 'fudge factor theory'. One of these motivations is to see ourselves as honest and honourable people, who will do the right thing. The other is to take advantage of opportunities to cheat and free ride on the efforts of other people. His experimental work shows that most individuals will take advantage of opportunities to cheat a little bit if they can. But they will not do this to the point of having to admit to themselves that they are dishonest and unprincipled. In other words most people cheat a little bit, but only a few cheat a lot because the latter is incompatible with a good self-image.

This suggests a mechanism which drives the phenomenon of giving misleading answers to interviewers. It is produced by 'cognitive dissonance' between the desire to vote on the one hand and social norms about voting on the other. Most people will recognise the social desirability norm, but the effect of this on their answers to interviewers depends on their sense of how important voting is to them personally. People who think that their own electoral participation is not that important may well recognise a social norm that voting is desirable, but they are less embarrassed to admit failing to meet this social standard because it is not personally important to them. But the psychology is different for those who really wanted to vote before the election and failed to do so, while at the same time thinking that voting is socially desirable. They face a strong internal conflict: voting is something they regard as socially desirable and personally important, yet they failed to act in accordance with these motives. One way of dealing with this dissonance is to mislead interviewers. Another is to mislead themselves, since many respondents may not be intentionally lying but rather end up convincing themselves that they voted even when they did not. Memories are notoriously faulty, and it is well established that people edit their recollections to suit their present self-image. However, only those who really value something go to such trouble, so when we try to assess whether respondents are giving 'socially desirable' responses in surveys, we have to know how important the particular topic is to respondents if we are to make sense of their answers. People only mislead when it matters.

FURTHER READING

The social desirability bias for voting is discussed in David E. Campbell's *Why We Vote* (Princeton University Press, 2006). Fudge factor theory is explained in Dan Ariely's *The (Honest) Truth About Dishonesty* (HarperCollins, 2012). The low levels of civic duty among young people are explored in *Affluence, Austerity and Electoral Change in Britain* by Paul Whiteley et al. (Cambridge University Press, 2013). Some of the interesting ways in which memory can deceive and people end up 'rewriting' history are discussed in Daniel Kahneman's *Thinking, Fast and Slow* (Allen Lane, 2011).

CHAPTER 6

Information matters: public support for overseas aid

Jennifer van Heerde-Hudson

When asked, British voters will tell you that roughly one in every five pounds spent by the UK government is spent on overseas aid. Europeans estimate aid spending at 10–15 per cent and Americans think – optimistically or pessimistically depending on how you look at it – that 25 per cent of the US federal budget is spent on foreign aid. In 2013, the UK government spent £11.2 billion, roughly 1.6 per cent of the national budget, on aid. In fact, with few exceptions, most rich democracies spend less than 1 per cent on aid.

Despite being a generally low-salience issue in British politics, overseas aid has become something of a feature on the national agenda, due, in part, to the coalition government's decision to ring-fence aid, alongside NHS spending, despite a wider move towards fiscal 'austerity' during the economic crisis; and a recent commitment by the government to a long-standing agreement by OECD Development Assistance Countries to spend 0.7 per cent of Gross National Income on aid.

Despite the increased public and political attention to aid, British voters continue to over-estimate the UK's commitment to poverty reduction. One recent survey asked respondents two questions: the proportion of the national budget they *think* the UK government spends on overseas aid, and how much *should* be spent on aid. The average estimate of spending was 18 per cent. Not everyone is completely wrong however; the modal or most commonly cited estimate was 1 per cent, and more than a third of respondents thought overseas aid spending accounted for less than 5 per cent of total spending. On average, respondents indicated spending should be about half (9 per cent) of what they thought was spent.

For aid advocates, this could be viewed as good news: although the public wildly over-estimates aid expenditure, they nevertheless prefer to spend much more than the current 1.6 per cent. It turns out, however, that the public doesn't want to spend very much on overseas aid at all. When given information as to *actual* spending levels, the public take the opportunity to restrain spending even further.

Given that more than 80 per cent of people thought aid spending accounted for more than 2 per cent of annual expenditure, you might expect that information on actual spending levels would increase support for aid expenditure when people were presented with the true picture. A reasonable hypothesis would be if 'John' *thinks* that 10 per cent of the budget is spent on aid, 5 per cent *should* be and 1.6 per cent *is* spent, John should support increased aid spending. Likewise, if 'Julie' *thinks* that 10 per cent of the budget is spent on aid, 1 per cent *should* be and 1.6 per cent *is* spent, Julie shouldn't support increased aid spending. But the public don't think like John or Julie.

In one recent survey experiment, respondents were randomly assigned to one of seven groups. The control group was prompted only to 'think about the amount of money the UK government spends on overseas aid'. In theory, respondents in this group should favour spending far less on aid, if like those respondents mentioned above, they wildly over-estimate actual aid spending. The other six groups were each given accurate information about current aid spending, using a variety of descriptions: the amount in pounds, in percentage terms, both combined, as pounds per £100 spent, and using visual aids.

So what happens to support for overseas aid spending when respondents are told how much is spent on aid? Very little. As the table shows, those in the control group (given no information on aid spending) had roughly the same level of support as those shown how much is spent comparatively, in either a pie or bar chart. Expressing spending as actual expenditure (£11.2 billion) or as a percentage of the budget (1.6 per cent) has no effect on support. Even framing aid in terms of pounds spent per £100 produces no statistically significant difference in support for aid spending. In other words, no matter how we talk about aid, the public generally supports decreasing aid expenditure.

INFORMATION AND SUPPORT FOR OVERSEAS AID SPENDING

	INCREASE A GREAT DEAL	INCREASE SOMEWHAT	STAY THE SAME	DECREASE SOMEWHAT	DECREASE A GREAT DEAL
Thinking about the amount of money the government spends on overseas aid ...	2	11	25	27	35
Thinking about the £11.2 billion ...	1	8	26	28	37
Thinking about the 1.6 per cent of the budget ...	1	7	30	26	35
Thinking about the 11.2 billion pounds or 1.6 per cent of the budget ...	4	5	23	27	41
Of every £100 the government spends, £1.60 is spent on overseas aid ...	3	8	25	33	31
The pie chart shows the percentage of the budget ...	2	10	29	32	28
The bar chart shows the percentage of the budget ...	2	9	25	32	32

Source: YouGov, 2013

While 'information matters' in the formation of opinion, it isn't the only factor. In the case of overseas aid, there is good evidence to suggest that perceptions of corruption and waste play a big role in driving attitudes and opinions: two-thirds of the British public think that we should not send aid to countries with corrupt governments; more than 90 per cent think every penny of aid should reach its intended targets and most think aid 'wasted'. Tackling the views of aid as wasted or likely to wind up in the hands of corrupt politicians would appear to be a prerequisite to increasing support. Second, the public discourse and media portrayal of aid is predominantly negative, and new information can't or simply doesn't override the strong negative images left in voters' minds. Simply talking about how 'little' is spent on overseas aid is not likely to be enough to move public opinion in the desired direction.

FURTHER READING

A summary review of public opinion and overseas aid can be found in Helen Milner and Dustin Tingley's 'Public Opinion and Foreign Aid' (*International Interactions*, 2013). A critical assessment of cross-national surveys of public opinion and aid can be found in David Hudson and Jennifer van Heerde-Hudson's 'A Mile Wide and an Inch Deep' (*International Journal of Development Education and Global Learning*, 2012). Andrew Darnton and Martin Kirk's *Finding Frames* report (2011) provides an excellent analysis of public engagement with aid.

—CHAPTER 7—

Wrong about nearly everything, but still rational: public opinion as a thermostat

Will Jennings

'**B**ritish public wrong about nearly everything, survey shows,' proclaimed a headline in *The Independent* in 2013, reporting findings from an Ipsos-MORI survey for the Royal Statistical Society. It found people thought 31 per cent of the population were immigrants, when the actual number was 13 per cent; that 58 per cent of people thought crime was rising, when in fact it was falling; and that people believed that £24 out of every £100 spent on benefits was claimed fraudulently, when the official figure was £0.70.

One of the perennial puzzles about the nature of mass opinion is how, despite the public knowing little about politics, and caring even less about the ebb and flow of public affairs, *collective* public opinion often turns out to be coherent and responsive to events and to new information. An influential line of research takes the view that while individuals may be ill-informed, public opinion in the aggregate is still 'rational', moving in response to events and changes in policy.

Perhaps the most persuasive explanation for this lies in the idea of public opinion as a 'thermostat'. The public may not have a good sense of what the government is actually doing but they are capable of making *relative* judgements of whether there is 'too much' or 'too little' government activity. This is an easier assessment to make than trying to understand the complex details of government policy. Voters simply observe the direction government is moving in, and react in the opposite direction. When policy-makers deliver *more* of something (such as more spending in a particular area), the public's demand for it decreases. When policy-makers deliver *less*, the public's demand increases (so voters react to spending cuts by demanding increased spending). The public regulates government activity like a thermostat regulates room temperature: when politicians turn up the heat, public demand shuts off; when politicians' interest in an issue cools, public anxieties heat up.

This idea of public opinion as a thermostat was developed by Christopher Wlezien using data on the responsiveness of public opinion to spending of the US government on defence, cities, education, the environment, health and welfare. Wlezien's study found substantial feedback from actual spending on the public's relative preference for more or less policy. For defence, for example, he showed that a 1 per cent increase in appropriations led to a reduction of 2.7 per cent in the proportion of the public desiring more over less spending. According to Wlezien, the public sends a consistent and meaningful signal about what it wants to policy-makers.

Similar to its preferences for spending, the public's attention to issues can at times seem capricious – being concerned about crime one month, focusing on the threat of Bird Flu the next, and turning to petrol prices the next. Yet the topics that are on people's minds are often a good indicator of the degree to which they are a problem. Consider unemployment. The Ipsos-MORI survey mentioned earlier found that, on average, the public thought the rate of unemployment

was twenty-two out of every hundred people of working age, when
the actual number was eight. If one plots the proportion of the British public in a given month naming unemployment as the 'most
important issue' facing the country against the actual unemployment rate this gives a very different picture, however. For the period
since 1979, this tracks the official unemployment figures remarkably
closely. Similar patterns are observed for the rate of inflation and the
number of working days lost due to industrial action as well, each
of which move in parallel with the relative emphasis placed on the
issue by the public.

UNEMPLOYMENT RATE AND SHARE OF VOTERS RATING UNEMPLOYMENT AS THE MOST IMPORTANT ISSUE FACING THE COUNTRY

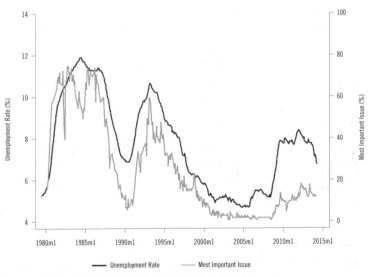

Source: Ipsos-MORI (most important issue), Office for National Statistics (unemployment)

So what underpins this process of opinion formation? It is possible to outline several ideas about why *uninformed* or *inattentive*

mass opinion may still be responsive to changes in policy or policy outcomes.

The first is simply that preferences or the problem status of issues are *relative*. People want more or less spending, or consider a particular issue to be more or less important than other issues. They do not need to know precisely the amount of policy they want to hold such preferences, just as someone who feels too cold doesn't need to know the precise temperature they want to be before putting the heating on.

The second is that on most issues the public receives a substantial amount of information either directly or indirectly about whether they are receiving more or less government activity in particular areas. Job figures, inflation, train delays, increases or cuts to public spending on hospitals are all regularly reported in the media. Of course in some areas the processing of this information can become severely distorted, to the extent that the relationship breaks down. Take crime, for example, where there is a long-standing gap between public perceptions of crime and the actual crime rate. Widespread distrust of official statistics means public opinion is not responsive to changes in policy or outcomes, or lags well behind then.

The third is that changes in aggregate opinion are not necessarily driven by the average citizen, who knows or cares little about policy, meaning that 'error' at the individual level cancels out. Movements in mass opinion can be driven by relatively small sections of the population ('opinion leaders') who possess the cognitive capacity to adjust their opinion in response to policy change in meaningful and systematic ways.

Despite people being poor judges of the actual level of policy and often holding incoherent views on issues, the ebbs and flows of mass opinion tend to reflect meaningful responses to events and to the rise and fall of problems on the agenda. It follows, then, that public opinion can exhibit 'rational' patterns of movement in relative terms, even when it is wrong about nearly everything in terms of the specifics.

FURTHER READING

The Royal Statistical Society study was reported in Jonathan Paige's 'British public wrong about nearly everything, survey shows' (*The Independent*, 9 July 2013). The idea of the public as a thermostat comes from Christopher Wlezien 'The Public as Thermostat: dynamics of Preferences for Spending' (*American Journal of Political Science*, 2005). The characteristics of polls about the 'most important issue' are discussed in Will Jennings and Christopher Wlezien's 'Distinguishing between Most Important Problems and Issues?' (*Public Opinion Quarterly*, 2011). The argument that aggregate opinion is driven by opinion leaders is put forward in *The Macro Polity* by Robert Erikson et al. (Cambridge University Press, 2002).

—CHAPTER 8—

When racism stopped being normal, but no one noticed: generational value change

Danny Dorling

How can you tell when the times are changing and great progress is being made, or when we instead appear to be going back in time – 'going back to '79', as the lyrics of a recent tribute to David Cameron's government suggested? Often it feels as if it was mostly in the past that great steps forward were taken. However, it was probably the case that at those times people did not realise that they were achieving much. The same may be true today.

Anxieties and social conflicts fuel a belief that Britain is becoming a less tolerant society. In some of the most unequal of rich countries, such as the UK and the US, benefit levels are now so low compared to average wages, that people will do almost any job, or more than one job, to avoid having to claim the new, very low dole. The government complains that immigrants will still do jobs locals won't. The environment is nasty and issues of immigration become highly ranked in what is most important at each forthcoming election.

In this environment you might expect people to become increasingly intolerant of others – people from different groups who could be taking 'their' jobs. The following graph challenges that assumption. It shows the slow but steady decline in opposition to mixed-race marriages, a good indicator of racial prejudice. A generation ago, in 1983, a majority of white British respondents expressed discomfort with the idea of having in-laws from a different race. By 2013, this figure had fallen to less than a quarter.

SHARE OF BRITISH RESPONDENTS EXPRESSING DISCOMFORT ABOUT AN ASIAN OR WEST INDIAN IN-LAW, 1983–2013 (%)

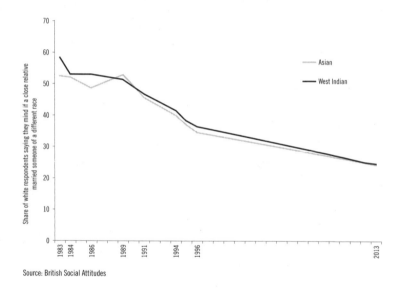

Source: British Social Attitudes

What the graph shows is that some things change slowly and steadily in a way that is almost impervious to immediate events. This is because much of this slow shift is produced by generational change. Older voters, whose views were shaped by growing up in an almost all-white Britain prior to larger-scale immigration, are very strongly opposed to inter-racial marriage – in 2013 over 40 per cent of those born before 1940 disapproved of it. Opposition is much lower among their children, born in the '60s, and vanishes almost entirely among their grandchildren: less than one in ten of those born in the '90s express any discomfort about having an in-law from a different race.

The graph shows that attitudes can become radically more tolerant even in times of rising inequality and social conflict. Hostility to minorities fell during the early '90s, despite a recession and mass unemployment, and fell in the 2000s despite the rise in BNP voting and widespread public anxiety about immigration. It is possible that the brief hiatus in the rise in tolerance in the mid '80s was related to the experience of mass unemployment and rapidly growing economic inequalities then, or a birth cohort effect, but what is most important about it is its brevity.

Your parents could well be among those who objected to mixed-race marriages. But if they were growing up in the Britain of the '40s then they were normal. Among younger people today few people worry about whether folk get married or not, or to whom – male or female, black or white. But not long ago it was as normal to be a bigot as not.

Exactly the same has been seen in the US. In the late '50s in the US, twenty-four people disapproved of mixed-race marriage for every one who approved. By the late '60s, that ratio had plummeted to 4:1. By 2012 the *approval* ratio had reached 6:1.

But have a little sympathy for your parents. Just look at what was common in the time of *their* parents, who grew up in a generation of British imperial rule, fascists ruling half of Europe and blackshirts marching in the streets in London. And now have a think about how the generations to come might view your generation. Look at how quickly attitudes are still changing. In a generation's time your views on whether we should worry about how few young men go to university or the sanctity of national borders or the theory that the very wealthy create jobs by investing their wealth could easily be perceived as a sad statement of the ignorance of our time. Whatever it turns out to be, it will be a view that is widespread today but will come to be seen as misguided in the near future.

Looking at past trends in changing attitudes helps us to see how much views that appear to be very fixed can change over the course of lifetimes and between generations. Politics often appears to be in a desperate mess. Progress is slow. Many things are getting worse. But we tend to concentrate on the bad news and on the most powerful, immediate crises. That is how we improve our political lives. We complain and agitate about what matters to us right now, even as other things continue to change and often improve. We might well look back in future at the years just before and after the 2008 economic crash and say: 'That was when the tide of social change began to accelerate.'

If the analysis of the figures above is right, especially in terms of recent US trends on public opinion, the tide may also be changing, not just in relation to the tolerance of mixed-race marriages and what that implies for the diminishing of racism, but perhaps also in many other areas that currently do *not* look encouraging in contemporary data. Whatever you think is true today ain't necessarily going to be so tomorrow.

FURTHER READING

This chapter is based on two articles that the author worked on in 2013: 'Tolerance, inequality and the recession' (Sheffield Political Economy Research Institute Blog, 2013) and 'It is necessarily so' (*Significance Magazine*, 2013), both of which use data from the USA. For a proper introduction you should read 'The Better Angels of Our Nature: How the Antiprejudice Norm Affects Policy and Party Preferences in Great Britain and Germany' by Scott Blinder et al. (*American Journal of Political Science*, 2013).

'A most wretched custom, assuredly, is our electioneering and scrambling for office.'

CICERO, 44BC

CHAPTER 9

The importance of economic sunshine: the economy and voting

David Sanders

In the 1992 US presidential election, James Carville, campaign manager for the Democratic presidential candidate Bill Clinton displayed on his office wall the slogan: 'The economy, stupid.' It was a continuing reminder that he needed to focus on economic issues if Clinton was going to win the election. Carville's insight was not new. Politicians and campaign strategists had understood for decades that they were more likely to win elections if they could promise a better economic future for voters.

Academics were not slow to realise that there were two interesting areas of research here. The first was to explore the way that politicians sought to manipulate the economy in order to ensure that economic good times were either present or just round the corner whenever an election is due. What became known as 'the political business cycle' involves looking at the way governments introduce difficult economic measures (tax increases and so on) fairly soon after their election in the hope that these measures will deliver medium-term economic benefits (such as higher economic growth) that will in turn feed through into people's pockets in time for the next election. In Britain, from the '60s through to the late '90s, governments of all political persuasions tended to use the eighteen months or so prior to an expected election to reduce interest rates, reduce taxation and increase government spending on public services.

The potential connection between people's economic perceptions and their voting choices generated the second area of academic interest – what is often called 'economic voting'. Distinctions were made between people's perceptions of their own and their families' interests ('egocentric' evaluations) and their broader views about the interests of the economy in general ('sociotropic' evaluations). Forward-looking ('prospective') evaluations were also distinguished from backward-looking ('retrospective') ones. Different academic observers stressed different sets of perceptions, but in Britain it was often found that prospective egocentric evaluations or 'personal economic expectations' correlated most strongly with voting preference. In other words, it was how people thought the economy would do in the future that mattered, not how things had gone in the past; and it was what the government would do for you and your family that mattered, not any judgement about the country as a whole.

For example, in the spring of 2005, when Labour was about to embark on its 2005 general election campaign, those who thought that their family's economic situation would get better over the next twelve months were overwhelmingly likely to support Labour (60 per cent), whereas only 16 per cent supported the Conservatives and 17 per cent the Lib Dems. But for those pessimistic about their family's outlook, the opposite applied: 45 per cent supported the Conservatives, 27 per cent the Lib Dems and only 16 per cent Labour. By 2013, with the Conservatives and Lib Dems in government, this position had been broadly reversed: optimists were overwhelmingly Conservative (56 per cent) and pessimists disproportionately either Labour (46 per cent) or Other (34 per cent). The Lib Dems weren't really popular with anyone in 2013, but their support among optimists was still almost twice as high as it was among pessimists. This tendency for economic optimists to support the incumbent government and for economic pessimists to support the parties of opposition has been observed in innumerable surveys at different times and in different countries. Even when lots of the other factors that are known to affect people's voting choices are controlled for (for example, their evaluations of leaders, their ideological positions and their socio-demographic characteristics), economic perceptions still appear to exert an effect on people's voting preferences. Indeed, taking full account of the effects of economic expectations can produce some surprising conclusions: several studies have found that the recovery of expectations that began in December 1981 was more important in determining the outcome of the 1983 general election than the successful military campaign in the Falklands in 1982.

AGGREGATE-LEVEL RELATIONSHIP BETWEEN GOVERNING PARTY POLL SHARE AND PERSONAL ECONOMIC EXPECTATIONS, 1979–2010

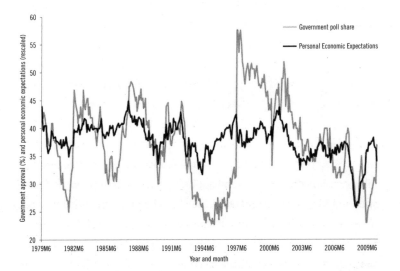

The relationship between government support and expectations also holds at the aggregate level. The figure shows the broad relationship between support for the incumbent party (the Conservatives from 1979 to April 1997 and for Labour thereafter, hence the leap in support April–May 1997) and personal economic expectations (the percentage of optimists minus the percentage of pessimists) between 1979 and 2010. The graphs do not match perfectly but they do tend to move together over time. There are certain periods when they match each other closely – as in the late '80s and early '90s. Indeed, the closeness of this relationship at that time enabled one study to produce forecasts of party support two years ahead of the 1992 general election which proved remarkably accurate. If governments can generate enough optimism through tax cuts and other ways of making people feel good about the economic future, then they can increase the number of people who want to preserve the political status quo that helped to generate their optimism in the first place.

But if this seems to offer a recipe for governments to keep winning elections simply by buying votes, there is an important caution to bear in mind. Economic optimism only converts into support for the government if people also believe that the governing party (or coalition of parties) is more *competent* than its rivals to manage the country's economic affairs. In some ways the most interesting part of the graph are the periods during which the relationship between economic optimism and support for the government breaks down.

During the '80s, the Conservatives enjoyed a huge lead over Labour in terms of public perceptions of their economic management competence, but that reputation for competence was fractured almost overnight by the Exchange Rate Mechanism crisis of September 1992. Even though economic optimism increased significantly after 1993, and even though that recovery of optimism produced only a modest rebound in Conservative support, the Conservatives' electoral chances were fatally weakened by the firm sense among the public that it was Labour that was now best able to *manage* the economy. Labour's lead on management competence continued through to the economic crisis of 2007/2008. Thereafter, the Conservatives reassumed their dominant position on competence; one that they have been able to maintain, notwithstanding all their other difficulties, in the period since. The return of economic optimism among many voters in 2013–14 may therefore be a cause for political optimism among Conservative and Liberal Democrat politicians; past evidence suggests they stand to gain if the economic sunshine returns.

FURTHER READING

A simple introduction to the subject can be found in 'Popularity Function Forecasts for the 2005 UK General Election' by David Sanders (*British Journal of Politics and International Relations,* 2005). An early forecasting study is 'Government Popularity and the Next General Election' also by David Sanders (*Political Quarterly,* 1991). An excellent review of the topic is provided in Michael S. Lewis-Beck's *Economics and Elections: The Major Western Democracies* (Michigan University Press, 1988). Recent important work is reported in *The Economic Vote: How Political and Economic Institutions Condition Election Results* by Ray Duch and Randolph Stevenson (Cambridge University Press, 2008); 'Reversing the Causal Arrow: The Political Conditioning of Economic Perceptions in the 2000–2004 US Presidential Election Cycle' by Geoffrey Evans and Mark Pickup (*Journal of Politics,* 2010); and *Affluence, Austerity and Electoral Change in Britain* by Paul Whiteley et al. (Cambridge University Press, 2013).

CHAPTER 10

Shamed into voting: how our nearest and dearest motivate us to turn out

Eline de Rooij

One of the things that puzzles political scientists is the fact that people vote. Political scientists find this puzzling not because of the much debated increase in political cynicism, but because they think voting is fundamentally irrational. Since it is very unlikely that any individual's vote will be decisive in determining the outcome of an election, each voter should realise that the outcome, for good or ill, is unlikely to be decided by their choice. They will benefit – or suffer – from the outcome whether they vote or not. So why do so many of them bother? In the last British general election in 2010, 65 per cent of registered voters voted and, although turnout at local elections tends to be lower, an average of four out of ten voters continue to cast their ballot.

One long-standing answer to this question has been that citizens perceive voting as their civic duty. We might vote not because we think we can actually affect the outcome, but because we feel we ought to. That is, we are complying with a widely accepted social norm. We live in a democracy and that requires that people vote.

But do individuals comply with such a norm because it makes them feel good about themselves (what is called 'intrinsic motivation') or because they feel good as a result of showing others that they are being 'good citizens' ('extrinsic motivation')?

One type of research that has started to test this uses field experiments, in which voter lists are used to randomly allocate registered voters into a treatment or a control group, akin to those used in medical trials. When properly done, randomisation ensures that at the start of the experiment there are no systematic differences between the two groups. Any subsequent intervention (or 'treatment'), such as contacting those in the treatment group and encouraging them to vote, can then be fully credited with causing any differences between the treatment and control groups in voter turnout rates after the election.

One of the best-known field experimental studies conducted in the United States suggests that the extrinsic motivation to comply with the norm of voting is much stronger than the intrinsic motivation. In other words, people vote because they worry about others' opinion of them. Alan Gerber and his colleagues found that individuals who received a piece of direct mail that simply appealed to their sense of civic duty were 1.8 percentage points more likely to turn out to vote than individuals who did not. So appeals to the individual conscience mattered, but only a little. Other individuals who received a piece of direct mail that, in addition, included their recent turnout history together with that of their household members and neighbours and noted that updated information would be sent to everyone in the neighbourhood after the election, were as much as 8.1 percentage points more likely to turn out to vote. A reminder that your neighbours can find out you stayed home on polling day acted as a powerful spur to casting a ballot.

Another American study showed that pointing out individuals' own voting records in recent elections motivated them to a greater extent to vote than informing them of the overall voting rate in their community. This implies that social norms have their strongest effect when we feel that others may be judging us as individuals, rather than when they may be judging the community we belong to.

In our day-to-day lives, this feeling of being monitored might be greatest within the confines of our own households. Who can apply social pressure more effectively than our own family members? Thus, some studies have looked at what are called the 'spill-over' effects of these experiments. The idea is simple: if social pressure influences one individual in a household, that pressure should spill over to others in the same household. One study in the US found that a doorstep canvassing campaign targeted at individuals living in two-voter households also had a substantial impact on the turnout of the household member who was not canvassed: 60 per cent of the effect of the campaign was passed on to the second household member. Although similar studies conducted in the UK are yet to be published, preliminary evidence from one study during the Police and Crime Commissioner elections in 2012 seems to suggest that spill-over also occurs within UK households. The study of the West Midlands contest showed that at least 84 per cent of the effect of a phone call encouraging individuals to vote was passed on to household members. A personal reminder to a voter seemed to work pretty well at motivating their partner and children as well, and worked best in households in which members supported different political parties.

We don't know what goes on at the proverbial kitchen table that makes us more likely to vote when our partner does. Do our partners exert social pressure? Do they remind us when and where to vote if we have forgotten amidst the many demands of our daily lives? Do they simply offer us a ride to the polling station when we are too lazy to go? Any or all of these things could be going on, but the net effect is the same: being made aware of relevant others in our lives monitoring our voting behaviour increases our chances of getting to the polling station on election day.

FURTHER READING

The best-known field experiment is 'Social Pressure and Voter Turnout: Evidence from a Large-scale Field Experiment' by Alan S. Gerber et al. (*American Political Science Review,* 2008) but see also 'Social Pressure, Descriptive Norms, and Voter Mobilization' by Costas Panagopolous et al. (*Political Behavior,* 2014). A brief review is 'Field Experiments on Political Behavior and Collective Action' by Eline de Rooij et al. (*Annual Review of Political Science,* 2009). Spill-over effects are examined in David W. Nickerson's 'Is Voting Contagious? Evidence from Two Field Experiments' (*American Political Science Review*, 2008). The UK evidence can be found in Florian Foos and Eline de Rooij's 'Household Partisan Composition and Voter Turnout: Investigating Experimental Spillover Effects between Cohabitants' (paper presented at the 72nd Midwest Political Science Association conference, 2014).

—CHAPTER 11—

Voting together:
why the household matters

David Cutts

O f all the contexts where people's identities, norms and attachments are shaped, it is the household that reigns supreme. It
is the main location for political discussion and decision-making,
and the primary context where individuals obtain and reinforce their
political values, norms and preferences.

People who live together are more likely to take their political cues
from one another and it is through such discussion that the social
norms of voting, or not voting, are established within families. This
leads to shared behaviour. When one person in a household votes
then, as a rule, so to do all the others: 'Those who live together vote
together.' More than nine out of ten people who lived in a multi-
person household where someone voted, voted themselves in the
2010 general election. Less than one in ten did so when living with
a non-voter. Of course, shared propensities to vote in families may
arise because those who live in the same household are more alike,
sharing socio-economic characteristics, values, attitudes and exposure to campaigning by parties. But even where household members
hold dissimilar attitudes, interpersonal interaction in the household

over time has been shown to weaken differences, with family members becoming more alike. A strong relationship still exists between the turnout and party choices of one household member and that of the others, even when accounting for their similar social backgrounds or political attitudes.

Some household relationships are more important than others and exposure to these varies through the course of life. There is strong evidence of a link between the political inclinations of husbands and wives, with spouses three times as influential as other relationships. The frequency of political discussion with a spouse also has a positive effect on voter turnout. Married people participate in greater proportions than those who are single, divorced, separated or living with a partner, as they have been found to place greater emphasis on traditional values such as civic duty. Married couples also have high levels of agreement which increase over time. As Chapter 10 shows, 'get out the vote studies' also find that the majority of any effect from voter mobilisation campaigns passes on to other members of the household. Unsurprisingly, the influence of parents over children is also well established, although mothers have a stronger effect on the political preferences of their offspring than fathers. In studies where both the mother and father support the same party, the child is three times as likely to support it too. Where only one parent selects a party, the child is up to ten times more likely to choose the same party as the mother than that of the father. This positive reciprocal relationship stems from the frequency of interaction, regularity of political discussion and the numerous learning opportunities with the mother.

The household is especially important for the socialisation of young people. The young are more easily influenced by others because they have not yet formed habits of voting or not voting, paying attention to politics or tuning it out. The majority of first-time voters live with their parents – the most important socialisation agents – and, as such, the decision of young first-time electors to vote is highly dependent on the participation of others in their family. This effect can be either positive or negative: disengaged parents produce disengaged offspring, while politically active parents pass on their enthusiasm just as effectively. A young first-time elector living in a house where another adult goes out to vote is over five times more likely to vote than a counterpart in a household where nobody else votes (the difference is much smaller for older electors). And these differences still exist even when socio-economic and even attitudinal influences are taken into account. It matters less whether there is one other voter or more than one; it is only necessary for most young people to have one other person around to help persuade them to vote.

The relative effect of living with another voter is much more important for first-time electors than for those in their twenties who have had previous opportunities to vote. This is a consequence of younger people moving away from their parents and living with others with whom they share weaker ties. But as voters enter their thirties and start families of their own, household influences on voting patterns start to increase again. The process once again goes into reverse as people enter the later stages of their life. Recent research suggests that voter turnout between the ages of sixty and ninety declines by more than 30 percentage points. And while worsening health is part of the explanation, the importance of the household once again comes to the fore. Older citizens tend to live alone more than the general population and so receive less social interaction and encouragement to vote from others. The decline in voting is faster for women, who are generally younger than their spouse and thus have a higher propensity to be widowed and live alone at an earlier age than men. Close intimates play a vital role in the participation process. Whether you are young or old, democracy begins at the kitchen table. Turning out to vote in elections is highly dependent on whether people live with other voters or not. Put simply, the household matters.

FURTHER READING

The discussion of which context matters in voting can be found in 'What Small Spatial Scales Are Relevant as Electoral Contexts for Individual Voters? The Importance of the Household on Turnout at the 2001 General Election' by David Cutts and Edward Fieldhouse (*American Journal of Political Science*, 2009). For the importance of the household on young people, see 'The Companion Effect: Household and Local Context and the Turnout of Young People' by the same authors (*Journal of Politics*, 2012). For the influence of the household on voting and partisanship, read *Partisan Families: The Social Logic of Bounded Partisanship in Germany and Britain* by Alan Zuckerman et al. (Cambridge University Press, 2007). On the effect of marriage, see David Denver's 'Another Reason to Support Marriage? Turnout and the Decline of Marriage in Britain' (*British Journal of Politics and International Relations*, 2008). For the turnout of senior voters, see Yosef Bhatti and Kasper Hansen's 'Retiring from Voting: Turnout among Senior Voters' (*Journal of Elections, Public Opinion and Parties*, 2012).

CHAPTER 12

One out of three ain't bad: the effects of low turnout

Cees van der Eijk

No election attracts all eligible voters to the polls, but the enthusiasm with which citizens exercise their right to vote differs considerably across contests. In the Scottish independence referendum, more than eight in ten voters went to the polls. In British elections for representative bodies the supply of voters is, by contrast, at its lowest in European Parliament elections, where it ranges from a low of 24 per cent (in 1999) to a 'high' of 39 per cent (in 2004). Most recently, in 2014, 34 per cent of voters – barely just over one in three – exercised their right to choose a member of the European Parliament.

One of the perennial questions triggered by low turnout is whether the outcome of the election would have been different had more people voted. If the parties' share of the vote would have been different with higher turnout, then the legitimacy of the election outcome as an expression of 'the people's' political preferences is in doubt. Moreover, low turnout could lead to those in power only serving the few who did vote. You hear this argument especially about young people – a notoriously low turnout group (as

Chapter 38 discusses) – and the argument that the low turnout of young voters made it electorally feasible, for example, for the government to triple university tuition fees. Implicit in this claim is the belief that those who turn out in smallest numbers have distinct interests that, if expressed at the ballot box, would lead to a different outcome.

So, what would have happened had more people cast their vote at the Euro elections? If the popular argument that abstention is a silent form of protest (in this case against the EU) is correct, then maybe UKIP would have done even better than they did. Or maybe not, if another popular argument is correct, namely that satisfaction with the status quo (in this case British EU membership) leads to inaction. Obviously, it is impossible to assess the validity of such speculation directly, for the simple reason that we cannot rerun the election with a different level of turnout. But we can get at the answer indirectly.

Opinion surveys allow us to learn all kinds of things about voters and non-voters which are not directly observable from the tally of the ballots. The British Election Study survey conducted immediately after the 2014 Euro election not only asked what people did in that election – whether or not they voted and, if they did, which party they supported – but also how they would vote if a general election had been held at that time. We can make use of this to estimate how the non-voters would have voted had they gone to the polls. We cannot directly use people's general election preferences as a substitute for what they might have done at the Euro elections, because many (approximately one in three) of those who voted in 2014 say they would vote differently in a general election to the way they did in the Euro election. But knowing the pattern of these differences between their preferences at general and European elections, and knowing how these patterns vary for different kinds of people, makes it possible to take into account how European choices differ from those in general elections – and then to apply this to respondents who did not vote in the European elections but who said how they would have voted in a general election.

This gives us a plausible estimate of the European election outcome if turnout had been at the customary level of a general election. This estimate is presented in the following table, along with the actual result.

You will see that for none of the parties does the estimate differ by more than 1 percentage point from the actual result and, in most cases, the difference is quite a bit less. Had turnout in 2014 been twice as large as it actually was, UKIP would have done slightly less well – but they would still have done well enough to top the poll. The same is true for Labour, and they would still have come second in the overall vote. The Conservatives would have come third (as they did), the Greens fourth (as they did) and the Liberal Democrats fifth (as they did). The ensemble of 'other' parties would collectively have done better by 1.5 percentage points but, given the fragmentation of this group and its low level of support, this would not have had any consequences in terms of who were elected as MEPs. In other words, if turnout in the European Parliament election had been at the level of general elections, the results, in terms of parties' vote shares, would have been virtually the same. This result also holds when doing the analyses separately for England, Scotland and Wales, to account for the nationalist parties.

ACTUAL 2014 EUROPEAN PARLIAMENT ELECTION RESULT AND FORECAST RESULT WITH TURNOUT DOUBLED

	ACTUAL 2014 EUROPEAN ELECTION OUTCOME (TURNOUT 34 PER CENT)	ESTIMATED OUTCOME AT 68 PER CENT TURNOUT (TWICE AS HIGH)
United Kingdom Independence Party (UKIP)	27.5	26.6
Labour	25.4	24.4
Conservative	23.9	23.6
Green Party	7.9	8.6
Liberal Democrat	6.9	7.2
Scottish National Party	2.5	2.2
British National Party (BNP)	1.1	1.2
Plaid Cymru	0.7	0.7
Other	4.1	5.6

These findings reflect what has been found in similar analyses of the consequences of low turnout in earlier European elections and in analyses of the same question using different methodologies: the effects of higher or lower levels of turnout are small when other things are the same.

The conclusion that the effect of low turnout on parties' vote shares is often negligible may seem surprising, but it should not be. After all, there was no British political party or movement campaigning for electoral abstention or electoral boycott. Also, no group among those eligible to vote in British elections is disenfranchised or discouraged from voting so that its particular interests and preferences cannot be expressed in elections. And finally, groups that vote at notoriously low levels, such as the young, are in many ways as diverse in their interests and preferences as the rest of the population. Under such circumstances there is little scope for turnout to have major partisan consequences.

The partisan consequences of low turnout may be negligible, but it does have other political consequences, which are not so innocuous. The act of voting engenders further voting. But so does failure to vote. Non-voting can be habit-forming too. Low turnout elections, like those for the European Parliament, thus contribute to the erosion of turnout in general elections. That is why we should be worried about them.

FURTHER READING

For earlier findings which reached very similar results, see Cees van der Eijk and Marcel van Egmond's 'Political effects of low turnout in national and European elections' (*Electoral Studies*, 2007) and 'The Electoral Consequences of Low Turnout in European Parliament Elections' by Cees van der Eijk et al. in *How Democracy Works* (Pallas – Amsterdam University Press, 2011). On the assessment of partisan consequences of low turnout by way of other approaches and on other types of elections, see the special issue of *Electoral Studies* (2007). For the detrimental impact of European elections on turnout in general elections see Mark Franklin and Sara Hobolt 'The Legacy of Lethargy: How Elections to the European Parliament Depress Turnout' (*Electoral Studies*, 2011).

—CHAPTER 13—

Too scared to switch: why voters' emotions matter

Markus Wagner

E motions have a bad name in politics. Voters who are seen as emotional are said to be swayed by appeals to their insecurities and prejudices, easily manipulated and just one step away from an uncontrollable mob. The ideal voter is often portrayed as one who thinks objectively and rationally about parties and policies, and takes their electoral decisions with due care and attention.

But this dichotomy between a cool, objective voter and an instinctive, emotional voter is a false one. We cannot divide our thinking into rational on the one hand and emotional on the other. Rather, emotions are always part of how we respond to the world around us.

Recent research in political psychology has identified two ways of thinking about emotions. The first is to distinguish positive from negative emotions. What we think about objects, events and people can make us experience positive feelings such as hope and enthusiasm: one example is how many Americans saw Barack Obama's candidacy in 2008. Sometimes, however, we experience negative feelings such as disgust, anger or fear: this is how some people react to gay marriage, immigration or economic insecurity. One important finding of this research is that negative emotions make us more rational: because we are uncertain and anxious, we look for new information, try to find out more about the threat we perceive, and take more careful decisions about how to respond to it. Negative emotions therefore make us less likely to act quickly and without caution; it's when we are feeling enthusiastic that we may be over-confident about the quality of our choices.

The second way of thinking about emotions is to look at each reaction as a distinct emotion. Anger is not the same as fear, which is not the same as disgust. A good example is the recent financial and economic crisis. The 2010 survey of the British Election Study (BES) included questions about voters' emotional reactions to the recession. Respondents could choose up to four emotions from a list of eight: angry, happy, disgusted, hopeful, uneasy, confident, afraid and proud.

Negative emotions predominated. The emotion selected most often was 'uneasy' (62 per cent of respondents), followed by 'angry' (50 per cent), 'disgusted' (39 per cent) and 'afraid' (31 per cent). But there is only limited overlap between these negative emotions: for instance, only 44 per cent of those who selected 'angry' also selected 'afraid'. Distinct emotional responses to the crisis were possible. While the actions of banks and governments that led to the worst recession in generations made many voters angry, other voters, scared that the economic problems would lead them to lose their jobs and their livelihood, were more afraid than angry. (Perhaps understandably, fewer than 12 per cent of participants chose one or more positive emotions.)

Blame plays an important part in determining these negative emotional reactions. Anger is a natural response if we hold someone responsible for a threatening event. A tree in your garden felled by a neighbour might make you angry, a tree felled by a storm less so. The influence of blame is especially strong if we think that the person or organisation responsible should have looked out for us and cared about our welfare instead of causing damage.

The financial crisis provides an illustration of this as well. The BES asked participants to identify who, if anyone, they held responsible for the crisis: the UK government, the EU, or international actors, for instance banks or the US government. Those who could identify a responsible actor were angrier than those who could not, so it is important whether or not we assign blame. Moreover, those who saw the UK government or the EU as responsible were angrier than those who blamed the banks or the US government. These are institutions that we help to elect and who are responsible for our welfare, so anger is perhaps an understandable response.

Different emotions also encourage different behaviours. Anger makes us want to remove the source of harm and leads us to engage in risk-seeking behaviour. This is what evolutionary psychologists call the 'approach system': angry people seek out the source of their anger, even at risk to themselves. But fear makes us pursue risk-averse behaviour and increases our vigilance. This is the 'avoidance system': people who are afraid try to escape the source of their fear.

Again the financial crisis gives a good example. The BES surveys, which measured voting behaviour in 2005 and 2010 as well as emotional reactions, show that loyalty to Labour differed depending on whether respondents were angry or afraid about the recession. Those who voted Labour in 2005 and who were angry about the crisis were 14 per cent less likely to vote Labour again in 2010 than those who were not. When explaining electoral decisions, 14 per cent is a big effect for a single factor. Importantly, this effect holds independent of Labour voters' perceptions of the economic situation in general and how the crisis affected them personally. In contrast, fear had no effect: previous Labour voters who were afraid about the crisis were not less likely to vote Labour again than those voters who were not. This fits with what we know about the impact of emotions: anger encourages people to take action against the source of their anger, so angry voters took out their anger on Labour by switching support. Fearful voters did not take action in the same way. These two emotions were both reasonable feelings to have about the dramatic and confusing events of 2007 and after, but they had very different effects on the decisions taken by the voters who felt them.

Our emotional reactions to events play a complex role in how we think about politics and how we take voting decisions. Having emotions does not turn voters into irrational, easily manipulated individuals. Emotions are unavoidable, and so we should not distinguish between rational, objective and thus 'good' decision-making and emotional, effect-driven and thus 'bad' decision-making.

FURTHER READING

For a general introduction to political psychology and a brief treatment of emotional reactions, see *Political Psychology: Neuroscience, Genetics, and Politics* by George E. Marcus (Oxford University Press, 2013). For the positive-negative emotions approach, see, for example, *Affective Intelligence and Political Judgment* by George E. Marcus et al. (University of Chicago Press, 2000); for the distinct emotions approach, see, for example, Jennifer S. Lerner and Dacher Keltner's 'Fear, Anger, and Risk' (*Journal of Personality and Social Psychology*, 2001). The findings on the financial crisis are published in Markus Wagner, 'Fear and Anger in Great Britain: Blame Assignment and Emotional Reactions to the Financial Crisis' (*Political Behavior*, 2014).

—CHAPTER 14—

Will joke, won't vote: the internet and political engagement

Marta Cantijoch

For two decades researchers and media pundits have discussed whether the internet is helping political parties and candidates extend their support base and mobilise citizens during election campaigns. On the whole, media pundits have tended to make excited pronouncements about the 'YouTube election' or the 'Twitter election', while the academic community has spoiled the fun by pouring cold water on the idea that the internet has (as yet) had a decisive effect on the democratic process. A key reason for scepticism has been the discovery that those who use the internet to participate in, or learn about, politics are mostly already political enthusiasts. Internet politics therefore tend to reflect the political inequalities which exist offline: in both spheres rich, white, middle-class, male university graduates are heavily over-represented.

This story of an internet revolution which, despite all the hype, has no impact at the ballot box, rests on a distinction between those who are inside the political process (on and offline) and those who are excluded. The former are motivated individuals who access information about the election, discuss it with their friends and family and might even help parties by donating money or volunteering. Most of these activities can be conducted either online or offline and engaged individuals will use whichever types are more convenient and accessible to them. In other words, the internet doesn't change what they do, just how they do it. Outsiders, by contrast, have little interest in politics or the electoral process. They feel no strong attachment to any political party, tend to mistrust politicians and don't have much confidence in the utility or effectiveness of political engagement. Most citizens in this group don't vote, and political activity on the internet won't change this as people have a great deal of control over what they consume on the internet. Those who find politics dull and alienating won't voluntarily consume political web material.

However, in recent years, a key finding from the latest studies of online campaigns in several democratic contexts, including the United Kingdom, suggests the emergence of a third category of person: the 'e-expressives'. These people share political opinions and election related material with others online, often commenting on the events of the day or even generating new material themselves. Today, during any election campaign the web sees an outburst of user-generated creativity running parallel to, and independent from, the official campaigns. Informal content produced by users such as pictures, jokes and video clips can easily be accessed and then shared to many others via social media platforms. A political statement posted on Facebook, a tweet (or retweet), a comment to a blog post, all can spur an online discussion among 'friends' or 'followers'. Many of these user-generated forms of political expression end up being more successful than official party-generated output. For example, while the most popular video on the Conservatives' YouTube channel has been seen under 200,000 times, a satirical clip uploaded during the 2010 general election campaign adapting Pulp's classic 'Common People' and depicting Cameron as an out-of-touch snob trying to relate to ordinary voters has been seen more than a million times.

It could be argued that this is not really a new form of participation but simply another online adaptation of a practice that already existed, just like online petitions are the digital equivalent of hand-signed petitions. After all, discussions and joking about the latest political advert or election debate have always taken place during election campaigns in pubs and around dining tables. But what makes the e-expressive mode original is that the opinions expressed can be heard by far more people, in less time, than the gripes of the local pub bore. The jokes and snark which best catch the national mood can rapidly go viral and be seen by hundreds of thousands, if not millions, of fellow citizens within a matter of hours.

Survey data collected by YouGov during the 2010 general election indicated that about a fifth of the electorate had watched unofficial videos about the election online, posted comments about it on blogs and social media, or shared unofficial online content with their friends. What makes this particularly interesting is that those who engaged most enthusiastically in these e-expressive activities were not the usual suspects who are typically involved in traditional political activity. The systematic political inequalities between political activists and unengaged citizens seem to vanish when it comes to the e-expressives: they are young people who do not feel closer to any party or trust politicians any more than the ordinary citizen. And while they engage with the electoral campaign with great enthusiasm, this does not seem to result in a greater willingness to vote on election day. They are enthusiastic commentators on the campaign fight, but are apparently not interested in influencing the outcome.

How can this be? If someone is making the effort to engage with, and publicly comment on, the campaign, why doesn't this process culminate in voting? Probably the best way to understand this is to realise that the distinctions often made between political insiders and outsiders no longer make much sense. Conceptions of what it means to be a good citizen are shifting, particularly among younger generations. The e-expressives are not traditional, dutiful voters. But nor are they simply apathetic and disaffected. They prefer their politics with a small 'p'. They enjoy expressing and sharing critical views, establishing loose and temporary connections with causes and around issues (even the electoral process if this is the topic of the day) without committing to formal groups like political parties. The digital environment appears to be an ideal platform from which to exercise this novel form of political engagement. And as this type of engagement becomes more popular, the political system faces a significant challenge. Adapting rigid political structures to accommodate this new style of citizenship will not be an easy task, particularly for mainstream political parties.

FURTHER READING

The first mention of an e-expressive mode of participation can be found in the studies by Eulalia Puig-i-Abril and Hernando Rojas (see, for example, *International Journal of Internet Science*, 2007, or *Journal of Computer-Mediated Communication*, 2009). Rachel Gibson and Marta Cantijoch explored how different, or similar, several forms of online and offline participation are, suggesting the novel nature of the e-expressive mode (*The Journal of Politics*, 2013). For more discussion on the changing nature of political participation on the internet among young people, see the special issue of *Information, Communication & Society* entitled 'The networked young citizen' (2014).

CHAPTER 15

One party can be the biggest winner and the biggest loser: tactical voting

Stephen D. Fisher

You have to be careful whom you vote for in the UK. Nearly all voters in other European countries can just vote for the party they like the most because seats are awarded roughly in proportion to votes, in voting systems known as 'proportional representation'.

It is less easy with Britain's first-past-the-post electoral system. If you are going to vote and try to influence the outcome, it is important to think about the relative chances that the different candidates have of winning your constituency. In particular, if you support a party that is likely to come third or lower you might want to consider voting for whichever of the top two candidates you prefer to stop the other from winning.

This is called tactical voting (or what Americans call 'strategic voting'). Lots of other types of behaviour also get labelled tactical voting, which can muddy the issue. For example, people may vote 'tactically' for small parties to help them gain a higher profile for future success or vote 'tactically' against their traditionally favoured party to limit their majority.

But since these involve different kinds of strategic calculation, it is better to call them something different to avoid confusion. The key elements of classic tactical voting in British elections are voting for a party that is not your favourite, and doing so in order to influence who wins in your constituency at the current election. So, there is both an act and a motive.

Like any good murder-mystery, though, there also has to be an opportunity, and opportunities to vote tactically in this way are pretty rare. To properly vote tactically you have to support a party that comes third or lower in your constituency, and less than a quarter of British voters are in that position. You also have to *know* (or at least think) that your party is coming third or lower locally. Even then, those who are relatively indifferent between the top two parties and strongly prefer a less well-placed candidate may not bother switching.

Despite all these barriers, on average over the last six elections about one in five of third-placed party supporters have switched tactically. But there are almost as many people again who say they are voting tactically but are switching the wrong way. That is, they say in a survey that they 'really preferred another party but it had no chance of winning in their constituency', but their preferred party actually ended up in the top two locally.

How could they get things so wrong? Most just misread the local political situation. This is fair enough since voters do not have much to go on. The only impartial evidence they have is the previous election result, which they have to look up for themselves, and since that was a long time ago they have to consider changes in the parties' national and local standings since. Voters struggling with this situation may also be swayed by leaflets from parties with conflicting and misleading claims about the likely outcome. Sometimes there is the added complication of boundary changes, which alter the local political context in unpredictable ways. So it is not surprising that many voters attempting to vote tactically make a hash of it.

Despite these obstacles, people get it right most of the time. The proportion of voters who misguidedly switch from one of the top two candidates in their constituency is small. The reason there end up being as many such wrong-way tactical votes as there are efficient ones is because there are many more top-two party supporters who might get it wrong than there are third-placed party supporters wanting to cast tactical votes.

This is an example of what academics call a 'base rate effect' and it is also the key to how the Conservatives both gain most, and lose most, from tactical voting. Of the three main Westminster parties the Tories are the biggest net recipients of tactical votes because they rarely come third in a constituency and so their supporters are rarely in the position where it would make sense for them to switch tactically away from them. In most seats the Conservatives come in the top two and pick up some tactical votes from those behind them, usually from Lib Dem supporters. The net result is that the Tories gain more tactical votes than they lose. Meanwhile, tactical voting from Labour to the Liberal Democrats is roughly balanced by tactical voting from the Liberal Democrats to Labour, and the Liberal Democrats are in third place or lower in more seats than either of the other two parties, so they end up net losers of tactical votes.

But in terms of seats, the effect on the Tories is negative. This is because of where the tactical votes go. Liberal Democrats do not give away their tactical votes equally: at recent general elections their supporters have tended to prefer Labour to the Conservatives. So in the Con–Lab and Lab–Con contests, tactical voting by Lib Dems on average helps Labour candidates more than Tory ones, and the difference is decisive in a significant number of seats. The story is even starker in the many Con–Lib or Lib–Con battles where the Lib Dems have picked up nearly all the tactical votes from third placed Labour supporters. There aren't enough other kinds of seats to redress the balance for the Conservatives, and so overall, because of tactical voting, Labour and the Liberal Democrats both win seats from the Conservatives, even though the Conservatives pick up more tactical votes overall. My colleague David Myatt and I estimated that in 1997 the Conservatives lost thirty-five seats to Labour and eleven to the Liberal Democrats as a result of tactical voting. Numbers in other recent elections are only slightly smaller.

Tactical voting is likely to be important again at the next election. At the time of writing the polls suggest the Liberal Democrats have lost over half the vote they had in 2010 and that support for UKIP has quintupled. If such dramatic changes are maintained into the election campaign it could be harder than ever for voters to assess the strategic situation in their constituency. Liberal Democrat MPs will doubtless be hoping that many of the large chunk of their former voters who currently say they would vote Labour will actually vote for them tactically, if not sincerely. The Conservatives might appeal for tactical votes from the UKIP supporters who would prefer a Tory-led government to a Labour one. But there is also likely to be some UKIP-to-Labour tactical switching. While the net effects of tactical voting on the parties are hard to predict, the 'base rate effect' discussed above, seems likely to strengthen: the greater uncertainty about constituency contests should lead to more mistakes, but there should also be more efficient tactical voting as a result of a greater number of third or lower placed party supporters with the opportunity to tactically loan out their support.

FURTHER READING

People commonly find it difficult to think about base rate effects and it often causes them to make predictions and logical errors (the base rate fallacy), even among those who have been trained to spot them, as Daniel Kahneman's excellent pop-psychology book *Thinking, Fast and Slow* demonstrates. The estimates for tactical voting from 1997 are in David P. Myatt and Stephen D. Fisher's 'Tactical Coordination in Plurality Electoral Systems' (*Oxford Review of Economic Policy*, 2002). A theory of how to analyse change in tactical voting between elections is set out in Stephen D. Fisher and John Curtice's 'Tactical Unwind? Changes in Party Preference Structure and Tactical Voting in Britain between 2001 and 2005' (*Journal of Elections, Public Opinion and Parties*, 2006). Broader issues are discussed in Stephen D. Fisher's 'Definition and measurement of tactical voting: The role of rational choice' (*British Journal of Political Science*, 2004).

CHAPTER 16

Don't trust your poll lead: how public opinion changes during referendum campaigns

Alan Renwick

Our politicians are increasingly enthusiastic about promising referendums. Indeed, on a range of constitutional matters, the convention is now that politicians have little choice but to call a referendum if they want to pursue change. Naturally enough, so far as they can, they want to hold only referendums that they are going to win.

But such votes sometimes deliver sharp surprises. Lib Dems pressed in 2010 for a referendum to change the electoral system because they believed public desire for political reform would carry the day, only to suffer humiliating defeat. In 2013, the Irish government held a referendum to abolish the Senate – a move that the polls had for years supported – only to see the pro-reform lead evaporate in the final months before the vote. The 2014 Scottish independence referendum, which many presumed would deliver an easy victory for the status quo, ended up going down to the wire.

So politicians and others need to get better at calculating their chances of winning, and at working out what they can do in a campaign to maximise these chances. To make such predictions, we need to know how and why public opinion changes in the course of a referendum campaign.

Research conducted by the Canadian political scientist, Larry LeDuc, combined with my own updates, reveals the general pattern.

The following figure shows the difference between the percentage of voters who say they will vote 'Yes' in pre-referendum polls (up to one month before polling day, ignoring the 'don't knows') and the percentage who actually vote 'Yes' in the referendum.

If the bar points down, that means support for 'Yes' goes down. If the bar points up, support for 'Yes' goes up.

DIFFERENCE BETWEEN SUPPORT FOR 'YES' IN PRE-REFERENDUM OPINION POLLS AND SUPPORT IN THE REFERENDUM (%)

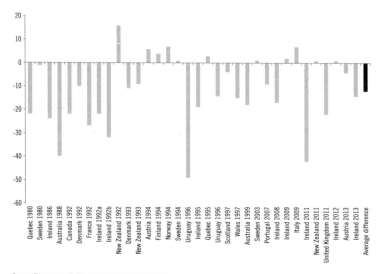

Source: Figures compiled by Lawrence LeDuc and the author

It is not difficult to see that support for the 'Yes' option – which almost always means the change option – goes down more often than it goes up. Of the thirty-four referendums shown, support for reform goes down in twenty-three and up in only eleven. Furthermore, the drops in support are typically much bigger than the rises: the total area of all the bars below the line is thirteen times greater than the area of the bars above.

That suggests that, unless you are already way ahead in the polls, you should be cautious of advocating a referendum on your pet reform idea.

But we can be more subtle in our analysis than that. Support for change generally falls as polling day approaches, but there are some exceptions. If we really want to know our chances of success, we will want to understand the exceptions as well as the rule.

Why does support for change generally fall? The main reason is that uncertain voters typically end up sticking with the devil they know. If you are unsure quite what effects a change will have, then it is safer to hold to the familiarity of the status quo. This mechanism is accentuated if the idea of reform sounds appealing at first blush; voters may respond positively to pollsters when they have not really thought the matter through, only for doubts to develop as they engage later. Examples of this abound. The most familiar in the UK is the electoral reform referendum of 2011. The idea of shaking up the political system, particularly after the expenses scandal, initially appealed to many voters; but as they engaged more, they worried about AV's possible implications, and most ended up voting 'No'. More strikingly still, Ireland's voters opted in October 2013 to retain their Senate even though polls had long shown a majority for abolition. Fear of empowering the government too far changed many minds.

What, then, explains the exceptions to these patterns? There are three basic reasons why support for reform may pick up steam. The first and most banal is that voters sometimes already know what they think well ahead of the vote. If opinion is already settled, scope for a drop in the 'Yes' vote is limited. The Scottish devolution referendum of 1997 provides a good example. It was, famously, the 'settled will' of the Scottish people that they should obtain a degree of self-government, and the polls barely changed throughout the referendum campaign.

Things get more interesting with the second reason. This is what is called 'reversion point reversal'. The 'reversion point' of a referendum is the situation that ensues following a 'No' vote. Generally, the reversion point is the status quo: if voters opt against change, then the pre-existing situation continues. But sometimes the pre-existing situation can successfully be painted as unsustainable. In several European countries, for example, voters, in being asked to vote a second time on an EU treaty that they had previously rejected, were warned that a second 'No' vote could jeopardise their country's position in the Union. Fear of the unknown now pushed voters towards a 'Yes' vote. Similarly, in four EU accession referendums in 1994, 'Yes' campaigners argued that, in a globalising post-Cold War world, isolation was an increasing danger and the old way of doing things was no longer an option.

The third and final mechanism is the anti-establishment bandwagon. If the establishment as a whole opposes reform and voters are in the mood to give it a kicking, a bandwagon for change can sometimes gather speed. This is particularly likely where the vote appears non-decisive and a protest vote therefore carries little danger. Such conditions applied in New Zealand in 1992 – the highest peak in our figure. The referendum was on electoral reform and most politicians united against it. Voters wished to express their anger over the behaviour of a political class that they thought was out of control. And the referendum was not decisive: a 'Yes' vote would simply trigger another referendum and a second chance to decide the following year.

If, therefore, you want to change the system and you are thinking about calling for a referendum to achieve it, beyond just looking at the current polling figures, you need to ask yourself three questions:

First, how firm is your support? Do poll respondents back you because they have thought about the issue and come to a clear view or just because the idea sounds nice? If the latter, expect your mouth-watering poll lead to evaporate.

Second, can you plausibly argue that the reform you want, while changing certain things for the better, will also protect aspects of the status quo that voters cherish? If you can, that could significantly boost your prospects.

Finally, are there any plausible bandwagon effects? Bandwagons are fickle: they can go one way or the other. So think about whether you can use them, but don't rely on them alone.

In the case of Scotland's independence referendum, the polls narrowed in the weeks and months before polling day. That happened because of deft use by the 'Yes' campaign of both reversion point reversal and bandwagon effects. Scottish First Minister Alex Salmond argued that independence would protect the National Health Service and other aspects of Scotland's social model from cutters and privatisers in Westminster. The pro-independence campaign successfully portrayed those who highlighted the uncertainties and risks of independence as members or dupes of a distant, arrogant elite who wanted to do Scotland down. In addition, in a referendum that sparked exceptional interest and passion, a positive 'we can really do this' bandwagon also emerged. Ultimately, however, it appears that those who made up their minds at the last moment plumped, on the whole, for the security of the status quo, and the

'No' side therefore won. The mechanisms that we see across most referendums therefore operated also in this dramatic case.

FURTHER READING

For Lawrence LeDuc's research, see his chapter 'Referendums and elections: how do campaigns differ?' in *Do Political Campaigns Matter? Campaign Effects in Elections and Referendums* (Routledge, 2001). The idea of the 'reversion point' is developed by Sara Binzer Hobolt in *Europe in Question: Referendums on European Integration* (Oxford University Press, 2009). For the dynamics of the UK referendum of 2011, see the special issue of *Electoral Studies* (2013) on 'The UK Electoral System Referendum, May 2011'.

CHAPTER 17

Two tower blocks in Dundee: constituency campaigning

David Denver

Back in 1970, John Bochel and I undertook a small experiment in Dundee. This was (we think) the first field experiment in British political science and the aim was to test whether local campaigning made a difference to election results. To do this, we selected two tower blocks of flats, situated in a safe Labour ward, equidistant from their polling station. With the co-operation of the local Labour Party – no other party did any campaigning – we canvassed the people in one block thoroughly and 'knocked up' supporters on polling day. Residents of the other received only a single leaflet from the candidate. A follow-up survey found that our 'experimental' block had a turnout 10 percentage points higher than the 'control' block (64 per cent to 54 per cent). Also, in the former Labour's share of the vote was 81 per cent; in the latter it was 77 per cent. These differences were magnified when we examined voters who had been canvassed more than once and/or 'knocked up' on polling day. Incidentally, in those days the flats concerned were seen as desirable places to live and were home to respectable families. They have since been demolished.

Although the results of our experiment were published, we (and a few others) remained voices in the wilderness in suggesting that constituency campaigning made a difference. What used to be called the 'orthodox' view of campaigning in Britain, established in the '50s by the Nuffield election studies, held sway then and did so for another twenty-five years. In this view, modern election campaigns were so dominated by the national mass media and the national party leaders that what happened on the ground in the constituencies was hardly worthy of consideration and certainly had no impact on election outcomes. The Nuffield studies were replete with references to local campaigning as a 'ritual' or even as 'anachronistic local rites'. This highly influential judgement was actually based on what now appears to be remarkably casual research. From the 1955 election onwards, the authors of successive studies asked regional party officials, in advance of the election, to identify constituencies in which their party's local campaign organisation would be particularly good or particularly bad. After the election it emerged that in almost every case electoral change in these constituencies ('swing') was little different from the average. It was concluded that local candidates and local campaigns were at the mercy of the national swing, determined by national factors, and that the many thousands of people who devoted time and energy to working in elections were worthy but somewhat eccentric individuals, maintaining a quaint but really rather pointless tradition. They might as well have stayed at home and watched television.

Since the '90s, however, things have changed remarkably. More rigorous academic research has produced much evidence that local campaigning is not just a 'ritual' but, for the most part, has an electoral payoff. These new studies of campaigning fall into two main types: those which relate some measure of campaign intensity across constituencies to election outcomes and those which are survey studies of the electorate.

The measures of campaign intensity used have been based on

surveys of election agents (who normally manage the local campaign on the candidate's behalf) and of party members. Campaign spending has also been used as an indicator of the strength of local campaigns. Although the studies using these approaches differ on some matters of detail and the measures themselves are not without problems, all have shown that parties' efforts pay off: more intense local campaigns produce better results for the parties concerned. As far as electorate surveys are concerned, it is instructive to note that the British Election Study (BES) report on the 1992 general election has a chapter called 'The election campaign' and within that a section on 'explaining campaign movements'. Nowhere in the chapter is there any reference to on-the-ground campaigning.

By 2001, however, after a new team took over the BES, the surveys included batteries of questions investigating exposure to face-to-face canvassing, telephone contact with parties and get-out-the-vote operations on polling day. The analysis found consistent evidence that these local campaign activities matter.

It should be said that no one is claiming constituency campaigning alone will reverse a clear national swing or that the impact is huge. In 2010, for example, the latest report based on a survey of agents suggested that an above average Liberal Democrat campaign could boost the party's vote share by 3.7 percentage points while for Labour the figure was 1.7 points and for the Conservatives just 0.8 points. Nonetheless, these are not increases to be sneered at in tight contests. Labour won six seats from the Conservatives by 1.7 points or less in 2010 and the Liberal Democrats seven by 3.7 points or less. If these had gone to the Conservatives then David Cameron would have been just seven seats short of an overall majority in the House of Commons.

Partly in response to the results of academic research on campaigning effects, party professionals now put much more effort into the constituency battles on the ground than before. Indeed, the 'ground war' is now central to the overall campaign strategy and the campaign activities of each party. In what are identified as key seats, the local effort is now seen as too important to be left to local enthusiasts and has changed dramatically since John Bochel and I tramped up and down stairs in our multi-storey blocks. Computers are now universally used for routine campaign tasks; canvassing (now 'voter ID') is increasingly undertaken by paid employees at central or regional 'telephone banks' rather than face-to-face on the doorstep; individual voters are targeted with direct mail shots organised from the centre. Outside of a few rural areas, public election meetings are virtually unheard of. Nonetheless, local campaigners are still visible on the ground. Leaflets are delivered and party number-takers with their familiar rosettes are still encountered outside polling stations while others, presumably, are crossing off the names of those who have voted and chasing up laggards. It is pleasing to report that they are not simply maintaining a quaint tradition but helping their party to maximise its electoral support. If any candidates dared to take the old orthodoxy at face value and decided not to bother with a local campaign then they would soon find out how much constituency campaigning matters.

FURTHER READING

The original Dundee experiment is reported in John Bochel and David Denver's 'Canvassing, Turnout and Party Support: An Experiment' (*British Journal of Political Science*, 1971). The 'breakthrough' book on constituency campaigning is *Modern Constituency Electioneering* by David Denver and Gordon Hands (Frank Cass, 1997). The most recent report based on surveys of election agents is 'The electoral effectiveness of constituency campaigning in the 2010 British general election: The "triumph" of Labour' by Justin Fisher et al. (*Electoral Studies*, 2011). The latter is not, however, for the statistically faint-hearted.

'All politics is local.'

USUALLY ATTRIBUTED TO TIP O'NEILL, SPEAKER OF THE
UNITED STATES HOUSE OF REPRESENTATIVES (1977–87),
BUT FIRST USED AS EARLY AS JULY 1932

—CHAPTER 18—

1859 and all that:
the enduring failure of
Welsh Conservatism

Roger Scully

1859: the year of the Austro-Sardinian war; the establishment of Queensland in Australia; and the first chiming of Big Ben. Lincoln's election as US President was still a year away; Queen Victoria's reign was only one-third completed.

1859 was also the last year, to date, when the Conservatives' general election vote share in Wales exceeded that in England. At *every* subsequent election, the Tories have done worse in Wales.

The direct consequence of enduring Conservative failure has been a persistently lopsided electoral politics in Wales. During the later nineteenth century and early years of the twentieth, the obverse of Tory weakness was Liberal strength. Even in difficult years, like the sweeping Conservative victories of 1886, 1895 and 1900, the Liberals remained supreme in Wales. In retrospect, harbingers of change can be seen in the two 1910 elections. Five Welsh Labour MPs were elected in both, and in the latter, the Liberals' vote share fell below 50 per cent, a level it would never again attain. The divisions that rended the Liberal Party after 1916 helped the substantial 1918 franchise expansion feed not Liberal strength, as pre-war observers might have expected, but Labour instead. With hindsight, Labour's rise can appear inevitable. That wasn't so at the time, and Wales (indeed Britain as a whole) experienced genuine three-party politics between the wars. But this period now appears an interregnum, not only between two cataclysmic conflicts, but between two eras of one-party dominance in Wales.

The 1945 election saw Labour emerge as Wales' dominant political force: winning a majority of Welsh votes and over two-thirds of MPs. Labour's 1945 landslide would not be replicated across the UK until 1997. But its dominance in Wales has proven persistent. At every subsequent general election, Labour has won the most votes, and a majority of the seats, in Wales.

But whoever has been strong in Wales, for over 150 years the Conservatives have been weak. From 1945 to 2010, their general election vote share was an average of 16.4 percentage points lower in Wales than England.

And while the Conservatives now do badly in other parts of the UK (such as Scotland and the north of England), within living memory Tory support barely differed between southern and northern England while a (bare) majority of Scots voted Conservative in 1955. Distinct to Wales is the historical consistency of anti-Conservatism. For almost as long as they have been able to vote, Welsh voters have shunned the Tories.

Conservative weakness has persisted through vastly changed economic circumstances. Wales was relatively prosperous in the decades preceding 1914, suffered in the appalling, inter-war 'locust' years, and has struggled with relative poverty ever since. Antipathy to the Conservatives has also long outlasted the main social movements that, some have argued, created and initially sustained it, such as non-conformist Protestantism, which opposed the Conservatives as the party of the Anglican church, and the industrial trade unions, which opposed the Conservatives as the party of capital.

While Wales may be poorer and more working-class than the rest of England, these social differences cannot remotely account for this exceptional voting pattern. Members of all major social groups in Wales (as, indeed, now in Scotland and northern England) are less likely to vote Conservative than their midlands and southern English counterparts.

Nor is Welsh exceptionalism a product of attitudes. Numerous studies indicate that people in Wales (and, again, in Scotland and northern England) are *not* more radical in their views than the bluer parts of England. Attitudes differ only about the parties themselves, with many in all of these regions appearing to view Conservatives as fundamentally alien.

Throughout the era of mass participation elections, Conservatives in Wales have been identified as a largely English party, somehow non-Welsh or even anti-Welsh in orientation, their limited electoral successes in Wales being confined almost entirely to the most heavily 'anglicised' areas. The Tories' opponents – first the Liberals, then Labour – more effectively identified themselves with ordinary Welsh people, including the many who were not 'nationalist' in terms of desiring greater Welsh political autonomy.

Some, in recent decades, have fought to develop a more authentically Welsh Conservatism – notably Wyn Roberts, Welsh Office Minister under Thatcher and Major, who produced the 1993 Welsh Language Act. But Roberts's efforts were undermined in the late '80s and '90s by the appointment of several Secretaries of State with little connection to (and, in one instance, very obviously no sympathy for) Wales. Nor were Welsh perceptions of the Tories obviously improved by their campaign for the first Welsh Assembly elections in 1999, which evinced continuing hostility to devolution and also the Welsh language. Things only began to improve somewhat after several Welsh Tories (notably Nick Bourne, National Assembly leader from 1999–2011) embraced devolution and sought to advance a more positive Welsh Conservative agenda. The 2010 general election saw the lowest post-war gap in Tory vote share between England and Wales (at 13.5 per cent) and the 2011 National Assembly election produced the Conservatives' best-ever result, overtaking Plaid Cymru to become the main opposition party.

Yet long-standing perceptions can be difficult to shift. Even in 2011, survey evidence showed that while Labour scored strongly in terms of perceived concern for all major social groups in Wales, the Conservatives were viewed as particularly concerned with the interests of the English. Moreover, the modest recent improvements in Welsh Conservative fortunes do not overturn many decades of one-party domination. Welsh politics remains seriously lop-sided.

Even prior to devolution, one-party dominance mattered for political life in Wales. Control of the Welsh Office periodically changed hands, but sustained Labour electoral supremacy produced organisational stagnation – highly uncompetitive elections in most areas did nothing to uphold vibrant party organisations. And one-party dominance now matters more directly for the government of Wales. By 2016, the Assembly will have completed four full terms, with no period of non-Labour government. The entire menu of options thus far has been Labour governing by itself, or Labour as senior coalition partner. The enduring weakness of Welsh Conservatism has substantially attenuated the centre-right's contribution to politics and policy-making in Wales. And, alongside Plaid Cymru's failure to sustain a serious challenge to Labour since 1999, it means that an end to Labour hegemony in Wales remains elusive.

FURTHER READING

The topic of this essay, like Welsh politics in general, is sparsely analysed. 'Why do the Conservatives always do (even) worse in Wales?' by Richard Wyn Jones et al. (*British Elections and Parties Review*, 2002) explores the Welsh Conservatives' long-standing electoral travails in more detail. Ian MacAllister's 'The dynamics of one-partyism' (*Llafur*, 1980) was written over thirty years ago, but remains relevant to understanding the implications of one-party domination for party politics in Wales. Peter Kellner's 'Why Northerners Don't Vote Tory' considers the Tories' more recent (but similar) difficulties in northern England.

CHAPTER 19

Of pandas, performance and parallel arenas: Scotland

Alistair Clark

There are, as the quip has it, more giant pandas in Edinburgh Zoo than Conservative MPs in Scotland. Tian Tian and Yang Guang outnumber David Mundell, the only Conservative MP. Given Scotland's recent referendum on independence, it is therefore a bit ironic that the avowedly unionist Conservative Party remains the only party to ever have achieved more than 50 per cent of the vote in Scotland, a feat they managed within living memory of some of the readers of this volume, in the 1955 general election.

Since then the Conservative vote has declined precipitously, the low ebb coming in 1997 when the party suffered the ignominy of returning no MPs at all from Scotland. But Scots do not only elect MPs to Westminster, they also elect MSPs to the Scottish Parliament, and they vote in very different ways for these two different institutions, as attested by the healthier cohort of fifteen Conservative MSPs returned to Holyrood in 2011.

One long-standing explanation for Scottish voting behaviour is national identity. The extent to which voters consider themselves either Scottish or British, or some combination thereof, has impacted upon voting behaviour, particularly since the rise of nationalist sentiment in the '60s. The SNP does best among those with Scottish identification. The SNP gained the support of 66 per cent of voters identifying as Scottish not British in 2011, and 49 per cent of those identifying as more Scottish than British. The Conservatives have been at the other end of the spectrum, with voters identifying as British, not Scottish, or more British than Scottish. Labour has tended to have quite a high proportion of voters identifying as equally Scottish and British.

MAIN PARTIES' VOTING OUTCOMES IN SCOTLAND 1999–2011: WESTMINSTER & SCOTTISH PARLIAMENT

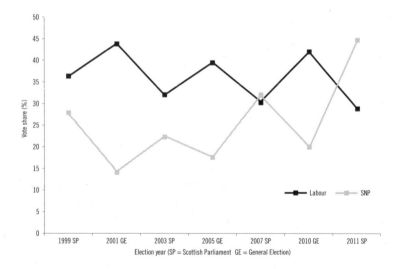

Not every vote for the SNP has been a vote for Scottish independence, however. Although 78 per cent of those in favour of independence voted SNP in 2007, in the previous two Scottish parliament elections in 1999 and 2003 this figure had been at around 58–62 per cent. The very size of the SNP's win in 2011, attracting many voters from Labour, suggests that this relationship weakened considerably from the previous round of Scottish elections in 2007. The key difficulty for the SNP is that they haven't historically been able to win elections in Scotland if they only appeal to those who want independence. The result of the 2014 independence referendum suggests this may well change in future Scottish elections. The key difficulty for Labour has been to ride both Scottish and British identities at once, a difficulty made acute by devolution and the SNP's ability to focus on Scotland uncomplicated by the need to appeal south of the border for votes.

Even more important is the extent to which Scots vote in different ways in different elections. In the 2010 general election, for example, the Labour Party won 42 per cent of the Scottish vote, while the SNP won 20 per cent. Just a year later, in the contest for the Scottish Parliament, the SNP won 44–45 per cent and Labour achieved 26–31 per cent on the two separate parts of the electoral system. Similar fluctuations have been seen when electing the two institutions since devolution began in 1999.

Sometimes such deviations are discovered because one of the elections is considered to be what political scientists call a 'second order' institution, in which the election is seen as relatively unimportant and a free hit for voters. By contrast, elections to the Scottish Parliament, which enjoys significant legislative powers, are not seen as a low stakes contest by Scottish voters. Scots think hard about who they believe will be most effective at Westminster and Holyrood, often arriving at different answers, and they vote accordingly.

In 2010, Scottish voters recognised returning a large bloc of Scottish Labour MPs was a more effective response to a Conservative resurgence than sending a small number of SNP MPs to sit on the sidelines. But in 2011, the SNP's relentless focus on their record of good governance since 2007, and Labour's ineffectual campaign and leadership, enabled the nationalists to secure 44 per cent of the vote from Scots who decided the party had the best ideas about running the country. This then led to the referendum on Scottish independence in September 2014, even though it is unlikely that the cause of independence was the top priority in the minds of most of those who backed the SNP in 2011.

It is therefore 'valence' or 'performance' politics which, in recent Scottish election studies, has become most important in explaining Scottish voting behaviour. This is academic speak for saying that, on issues where there is some broad cross-party agreement such as the general need for economic growth, voters will choose by assessing who they think is best placed to deliver the goods. Often voters in search of a shortcut do this by focusing on the parties' leaders. Often highly complex statistical arguments lead to the rather simple conclusion that many of the Scots who helped the SNP achieve a landslide victory in 2011 did so because they thought Alex Salmond was good at running the country and should continue doing so.

Since devolution, Scotland has also been a testing bed for electoral systems. Scots elect local and regional MSPs under a broadly proportional two-tier system and, when choosing their councillors, they rank the choices available under a system called Single Transferable Vote (also used in both parts of Ireland). Consequently, Scots are now used to being able to register multiple preferences, rank parties and split their tickets, something English voters outside London or the few localities where Mayors are directly elected, have no opportunity to do. Estimates suggest that around 20 per cent of Scottish voters split their ballot papers between two parties in early Scottish Parliament elections. A party such as the Greens could not be elected were this not the case as they only contest the proportional regional list seats on the AMS voting system. Independent candidates, flamboyant socialists and a Pensioners' Party have all won election via the regional list, while in local elections voters can, and do, transfer votes between parties from all parts of the Scottish political spectrum.

The main Scottish parties have become 'catch-all' parties, with similar electorates drawn from across Scottish society. National identity remains important but parties' competence and performance in the different arenas open to Scottish voters is also crucial in explaining voting behaviour in Scotland and its outcomes at Holyrood and Westminster.

How Edinburgh's pandas view Scottish politics is unknown, but in emphasising the performance and competence of the party choices they have before them, voters in Scotland may not be as different to voters elsewhere in Britain as they like to think, even if the outcomes may well be more eye-catching.

FURTHER READING

There have been many studies of Scottish voting behaviour. Recent elections have been most dramatic. For the 2007 election, see *Revolution or Evolution? The 2007 Scottish Elections* by John Curtice et al. (Edinburgh University Press, 2009) and for the SNP's dramatic victory in 2011 see *More Scottish than British? The 2011 Scottish Parliament Election* by Chris Carman et al. (Palgrave, 2014). On local elections under the single transferable vote see 'Voter Reactions to a Preferential Ballot: The 2007 Scottish Local Elections' by David Denver et al. (*Journal of Elections, Public Opinion and Parties*, 2009) and Alistair Clark's 'Second Time Lucky? The Continuing Adaptation of Parties and Voters to the Single Transferable Vote in Scotland' (*Representation*, 2013).

—CHAPTER 20—

The myth of meritocratic Scotland: political cultures in the UK

Ailsa Henderson

Successive election manifestos from political parties in Scotland have argued that Scots have different values to those in the rest of the UK. More meritocratic, more communitarian, more supportive of state intervention in the economy and EU membership, Scots are portrayed as a left-leaning social democratic foil to an essentially conservative, Eurosceptic, class-bound England. Such comparisons were rife during the Thatcher years but have continued today and feature regularly in the claims made by politicians and parties. Devolution, argued the Labour Party, would allow Scots to turn their distinct preferences into practice. Independence, argued the SNP repeatedly during the independence referendum campaign, would allow them to do so without the risk of intervention from London.

If we actually look at what people in Scotland, Wales and England think about various policy options or fundamental values we can often identify clear distinctions among them. They back different parties in elections, they hold different national identities. They vary in how well they perceive the current political system to be working (does Scotland/Wales/England get its 'fair share'?) and in the constitutional solutions that they propose. Attitudes to Europe are slightly different: Scottish voters are more supportive of the European Union, on some measures at least. But even with Europe the differences depend on the survey and the particular question asked. The 2013 British Social Attitudes Survey shows few significant differences across Scotland, England and Wales on whether to stay in the EU while the 2014 Future of England Survey shows Scots are significantly more likely to believe membership in the EU is 'a good thing'.

Much of the rhetoric about distinct political cultures concerns fundamental economic and social values: whether a state should be interventionist or not; whether women with young children should work outside the home; whether the state should support censorship in certain circumstances or ensure resources are redistributed from the rich to poor. On these sorts of issues, and on fundamental evaluations of the state (our sense of trust and sense of efficacy), the claims of distinctiveness typically outstrip results. Scots are not more meritocratic or communitarian than English or Welsh residents. Even where there are differences, they fade once you control for demographic characteristics such as social class. Scots feel differently about the UK, about how well it runs and how it should organise itself, but they don't necessarily feel differently about how a state in general should operate and what it should do for people.

The table provides average scores (taken from multiple questions) for three typical measures: a welfarism scale (with higher scores implying support for a more interventionist state); a libertarian–authoritarian scale (higher scores implying greater support for censorship); and a left–right scale (higher scores implying more right-wing). In no case are there significant differences between Scotland, Wales and England.

COMMON VALUES ACROSS SCOTLAND, WALES AND ENGLAND

	SCOTLAND	WALES	ENGLAND
WELFARISM (higher scores imply more support for welfare)	2.68 (1.57)	2.53 (1.72)	2.67 (1.75)
LIBERTARIAN–AUTHORITARIAN (higher scores imply support for censorship)	3.37 (1.61)	3.25 (1.83)	3.27 (1.88)
LEFT–RIGHT (higher scores imply support for industry, not redistribution)	2.17 (1.45)	1.99 (1.50)	2.21 (1.71)

Results are mean scores with standard deviations in parentheses.

So where do these claims of distinct political cultures come from? Some researchers have long argued that this is a north Britain–south Britain divide, that values still have more to do with social demographic factors such as one's social class, gender or age, and that the distribution of people in different economic circumstances is driving regionalised pockets of support for different values or different policies. There is much merit to this argument.

At the same time, the presence of a Scottish Parliament and a Welsh Assembly means that Scottish and Welsh political parties have a venue in which to articulate perceived differences in values and to legislate on their behalf. And so the perception of value differences between countries, even if it is misleading, can lead to real differences in policy. Legislators who believe in a more communitarian or left-wing Scotland have used such arguments to justify introducing free university education and free personal care for the elderly in Scotland. Perhaps, therefore, the more politically important feature of these distinct values across the regions of the UK is not whether they are true, but whether they are perceived to be true.

This distinction between evidence and perception helps to explain the sometimes contradictory results we see in surveys and the arguments among politicians about whether Scottish, Welsh, English or indeed British values exist. When asked to describe whether they are more left- or right-wing, Scots, for example, are significantly more likely to report themselves as being left-wing than other Britons. But when we ask about the types of values that would indicate whether someone is left-wing or not, there aren't usually meaningful differences across the regions of Britain. The 2014 Future of England Survey asked about basic attitudes to immigration and legalising same-sex marriage, as well as whether people thought attitudes in their 'region' were more supportive of each of these policies than elsewhere in the UK. The Scottish answers are revealing: although Scottish attitudes are actually similar to those in England and Wales, Scots believe that they are more in favour of these policies than they are and the gap between actual attitudes and perceived attitudes is larger in Scotland than in any other part of Britain. So Scots believe they are distinctively left-wing, their belief in this distinctiveness is reinforced by the rhetoric from politicians and civic organisations, and it then comes to form part of the mental imagery of Scottish national identity. If being a Scot is less about where you were born and more about the values you hold, does it matter if such distinctive 'Scottish' values don't really exist? And for whom are legislators creating policy: the electors they have, or the electors they think they have? If politicians create legislation based on what they believe their voters value, rather than what they actually value, do they end up creating the electorate they imagine? 'Scottish values' may be more imagined than real right now, but several decades of legislation seeking to reflect such values could create the distinct political culture it currently seeks to reflect.

FURTHER READING

The political culture classic remains Gabriel Almond and Sidney Verba's *The Civic Culture* (Princeton University Press, 1963) and still provides interesting reading on political culture in the UK. The British and Scottish Social Attitudes surveys have generated a number of useful chapters on the nature of regional variations in attitudes, for example John Curtice's 'One Nation Again' in *British Social Attitudes 13* (Dartmouth, 1996). For an account of Scottish political culture and its role in the national debate see Ailsa Henderson's *Hierarchies of Belonging: National Identity and Political Culture in Scotland and Quebec* (McGill-Queen's University Press, 2007). The most recent accounts of English political culture may be found in the Future of England reports: *The Dog That Finally Barked* (IPPR, 2012) and *England and its Two Unions* (IPPR, 2013), both by Richard Wyn Jones et al. For Scotland and Wales, useful publications resulting from election studies are *More Scottish than British* by Chris Carman et al. (Palgrave, 2014) and *Wales Says Yes* by Richard Wyn Jones and Roger Scully (University of Wales Press, 2012).

— CHAPTER 21 —

Richard Dawkins, look away now: religion and electoral choice in Northern Ireland

Jon Tonge

Northern Ireland could make a reasonable claim to have more elected representatives per voter than any place on Earth. Its electorate of 1.2 million is represented by 108 Assembly members, eighteen MPs, three MEPs and a staggering 462 councillors, a figure mercifully reduced recently from 582. At one point they were joined by sixty members of a 'Civic Forum' at Stormont, although somehow Northern Ireland has got by without them since 2002. There are even two First Ministers. The 'Deputy First Minister' has the same status as the 'First Minister', although that did not stop Ian Paisley, as the 'real' First Minister, referring to Sinn Fein's Martin McGuinness as 'My Deputy'.

Considering fewer than 700,000 people vote in Northern Ireland elections, the political party-to-voter ratio is similarly impressive. The Unionist electorate alone can pick from, in order of current importance, the Democratic Unionist Party (DUP), the Ulster Unionist Party (UUP), the Traditional Unionist Voice, the Progressive Unionist Party and NI21 (NI21 doesn't call itself Unionist, but it is). Nationalists have to make do with two parties at present: Sinn Fein, dominant since 2001, and the Social Democratic and Labour Party (SDLP), plus some independent republicans.

The region's plethora of rulers govern a polity whose title is not agreed. Sinn Fein's elected representatives decline to recognise the term 'Northern Ireland', preferring 'the North of Ireland' or the 'Six Counties' (the previous term was 'Occupied' Six Counties, so things are moderating).

The 1998 Good Friday Agreement did away with most political violence, of course – apart from the 2,800+ shooting and bombing incidents and over 150 deaths since. These figures may look grim, but they represent an 80 per cent improvement on 1970–97. But despite the reduction in political violence, and some notable shifts in attitudes to constitutional issues (only one-third of Catholics now definitely want a united Ireland, according to survey evidence), Northern Irish voters remain, in party terms, as divided as ever when they cast their ballots.

Ethno-national division and a sectarian chasm continue to dominate all of Northern Ireland's many elections. Most electors do not identify as 'Northern Irish', only one-quarter adopting the label, more preferring to be seen as 'British' or 'Irish'. Effectively there are separate communal elections for each contest, one within the Protestant Unionist British tradition; the other within the Catholic Nationalist Irish community, one of the strongest relationships between religion and party choice anywhere in Europe.

At the last general election, the correlation between the total vote for Nationalist parties and the percentage of Catholics in each constituency was 0.987. For the non-statistically minded reader, 1.000 would represent a perfect match, so we are not far away. On the

Protestant side, the equivalent score (related to votes for Unionist parties obviously) was 0.943.

The most recent (2012) Northern Ireland Life and Times survey found that only 1 per cent of Protestants described themselves as 'Nationalist', while the percentage of Catholics describing themselves as Unionist was a fairly emphatic 0 per cent. Curiously, despite this zero, 1 per cent of Catholics admitted to supporting the Democratic Unionist Party, although no Protestants admitted to voting Sinn Fein. Unionist and Nationalist parties have an almost exclusively single-religion base. For example, Catholic membership of the DUP is a mere 0.6 per cent.

According to successive Life and Times surveys, the largest single category of elector (over 40 per cent) in Northern Ireland is one who loftily declares him/herself to be neither Unionist nor Nationalist. But 90 per cent of votes are for Unionist or Nationalist parties. The non-aligned Alliance only wins a low single digit share. Avowedly non-Unionist, non-Nationalist electors seem either to be the least likely to vote – or the least likely to tell the truth to survey researchers.

An electoral Spring remains elusive. Westminster's plurality first-past-the-post elections may reinforce this communal voting model, by encouraging voters on both sides of the divide to consolidate behind a single sectarian candidate, but there is at least the *potential* for lower preference vote transfers across the sectarian divide under the more proportional Single Transferable Vote method used for all other contests. However, the traffic across the divide – Protestants voting for Nationalist parties or Catholics voting for Unionist parties – remains pitifully low. The table shows the low rate of cross-community lower preference vote transfers since the Assembly was created in 1998.

LOWER PREFERENCE VOTE TRANSFERS ACROSS THE SECTARIAN DIVIDE IN NORTHERN IRELAND, 1998–2011 ASSEMBLY ELECTIONS, AS PERCENTAGE OF AVAILABLE VOTE TRANSFERS

TRANSFER FROM	TRANSFER TO	PERCENTAGE OF AVAILABLE VOTE TRANSFERS
DUP	Sinn Fein	0.2
UUP	Sinn Fein	0.3
DUP	SDLP	4.9
UUP	SDLP	7.9
Sinn Fein	DUP	0.3
Sinn Fein	UUP	0.3
SDLP	DUP	1.4
SDLP	UUP	12.8

Obviously there are more important aspects of communal division than reluctance to transfer lower preference votes across a sectarian chasm: the percentages of Northern Ireland's population in 'mixed' marriages, or children attending religiously integrated schools, are both in single figures, for starters.

There is, however, one way in which the two communities *are* beginning to unite in electoral terms. During the troubles, Northern Ireland had the highest turnout in the UK. But turnout has been falling in all types of Northern Ireland election over the last decade and at the 2010 general election Northern Ireland had the lowest turnout in the country. In other countries, low turnout may be frowned upon, but in Northern Ireland it may have a more benign interpretation.

The two communities have not turned away from the ballot box to the same degree – Catholics are more likely to vote than Protestants (turnout is 6 per cent higher in majority Nationalist seats and even middle-class Protestants have a tendency to ignore elections)

– but both communities are at least beginning to unite in eschewing the ballot box.

FURTHER READING

Northern Ireland's electoral polarity – and how religious affiliation, not class, shapes allegiance – is detailed in Jocelyn Evans and Jon Tonge's 'Social Class and Party Choice in Northern Ireland's Ethnic Blocs' (*West European Politics*, 2009). A gentler, election-specific, guide is provided by the same authors in their chapter 'Northern Ireland' in *Britain Votes 2010* (Oxford University Press, 2010). For more on Northern Ireland's power-sharing and parties, see John McGarry and Brendan O'Leary's *The Northern Ireland Conflict: Consociational Engagements* (Oxford University Press, 2004). Annual surveys of Northern Ireland opinion are available via the Northern Ireland Life and Times surveys.

CHAPTER 22

North and south: political geography

Charles Pattie

The fundamental geographic division in modern British elections is well known. Conservative MPs overwhelmingly represent southern England outside London: those constituencies elect 31 per cent of all British MPs but in 2010 accounted for 53 per cent of Conservative MPs. In contrast, Scotland, Wales, and the north of England provided 41 per cent of all MPs, but just 17 per cent of the Conservatives'. Major northern cities such as Birmingham, Liverpool, Sheffield, Manchester, Newcastle, Leeds and Bradford elected no Conservatives at all in 2010, and several had no Conservatives on their city councils either.

But it's not just the Conservatives who are geographically concentrated. Two-thirds of Labour's current MPs were elected from Scotland (forty-one), Wales (twenty-six) and the north of England (104). Just ten represent constituencies in East Anglia and the south outside London. Even the Liberal Democrats, often thought of as less regionally concentrated, draw nearly half of their current MPs from the south west (fifteen out of the region's fifty-five) and Scotland (eleven out of fifty-nine), but barely feature in the

English midlands, where they won just two of the 105 seats. Only London – where all three parties do relatively well – breaks this north–south divide.

It hasn't always been like this. In 1951, almost half Scotland's votes and seats went to the Conservatives, as did 36 per cent of the seats in the major northern cities, while in the south and east outside London Labour won 42 per cent of the vote (though only 17 per cent of the seats). The figure shows the difference between the Conservatives' and Labour's percentage shares of the vote in each region in 1951 and 2010. Where the Conservatives lead over Labour, the difference is positive: where they trail it is negative. The charts tell a story of a nation dividing: in every region, except London and Wales, the political divide yawns wider in 2010 than it did in 1951. An almost identical pattern can also be seen in the distribution of seats.

DIFFERENCE BETWEEN CONSERVATIVE AND LABOUR VOTE PERCENTAGES BY REGION, 1951 AND 2010

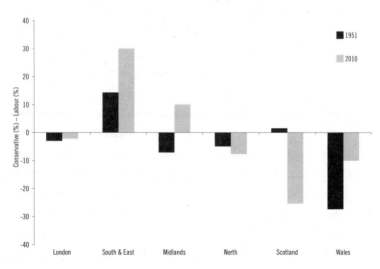

This geographical polarisation partly reflects deep social changes. In the '50s, tensions between Roman Catholics (many of Irish descent) and Protestants still influenced politics in the west of Scotland and north-west England. The Conservatives campaigned as Unionists, in the sense of uniting the UK, giving them an important Protestant working-class support base. But outside Northern Ireland these tensions lost their purchase in the second half of the twentieth century, diminishing Conservative support. Similarly, the class basis of voting in mid-twentieth century Britain contributed to the electoral geography, as Labour built its strength in the working-class communities of the northern industrial centres, while the Conservatives appealed to more middle-class suburban, rural and southern communities.

But the geography of class cannot explain rapid fluctuations in the regional electoral divide since the late '70s, because class geographies do not change that quickly, and in any case class is no longer such a major influence on vote. A stronger explanation is Britain's changing economic geography. Economic restructuring in the '70s and '80s hit the mining and manufacturing areas of the midlands and north particularly hard, while financial services fuelled a boom in southern England. The consequence was that support for the incumbent Conservative government grew in the prosperous south but declined in the faltering north, while support for the Labour opposition shifted in the opposite direction, widening the gap. (In 1987 the Conservative vote was 56 per cent in the south east outside London, but just 37 per cent in the north of England: Labour's shares were 17 per cent and 42 per cent.) When a housing slump in the early '90s hit property values and household wealth in the south, however, the Conservative government's support there waned, narrowing the gap again – by 1997, the Conservative vote was 41 per cent in the south east and 26 per cent in the north: Labour's vote grew in both regions, to 32 per cent and 55 per cent respectively. The electoral divide continued to narrow for some years under the New Labour government elected in 1997, which presided over a prolonged period of growth for most of the UK. But when the economy slumped in 2008, the north–south regional economic and political divide widened again; by 2010, Labour won 17 per cent in the south east and 38 per cent in the north: the Conservatives took 50 per cent and 31 per cent.

Building on the Liberals' post-1970 revival, the Liberal Democrats used the north–south divide to create opportunities for themselves at both ends of the country. In many northern cities, they replaced the Conservatives as the main alternative to Labour, while in much of the south they replaced Labour as the main alternative to incumbent Conservatives. This further eroded each of the 'big two' parties' footholds in their weaker regions. Within England, this resulted not in a country-wide three-party system but rather three two-party systems concentrated in different regions: in Scotland, the SNP became Labour's main rival.

This all has important consequences for party strategy. In the '80s, Labour was increasingly restricted to its northern urban strongholds and had no prospect of majority government. To win back power, the party had to convince voters further south that it could deliver economic prosperity. Achieving this was key to New Labour's three Westminster majorities in 1997–2005. Only when economic crisis post-2007 undermined Labour's reputation for competence did the party lose sufficient ground in the south and midlands to push it from office, ground that has to be recovered to ensure success in 2015. The Conservatives, too, face a strategic geographical problem. Now a marginal force in the English urban north, Scotland and Wales, they could still form majority governments based on support in the south and midlands (though this would not be easy), but the party's credentials as a UK-wide force are compromised.

But perhaps the most important consequence of regional political polarisation has been the steep decline in the number of marginal constituencies. In the early '50s, 25–30 per cent of all constituencies were Conservative/Labour marginals, in which less than 10 percentage points separated the two parties. By 2010, this had halved to just 15 per cent of seats. Fewer marginals mean a less responsive electoral system (with larger swings in national vote shares required to unseat incumbent governments) as well as an increasing concentration of campaign effort on a few voters in a few key places. As the country becomes politically more divided, the incentives of party competition encourage politicians to talk to ever smaller and more localised groups of voters. As the United Kingdom divides, so fewer places matter.

FURTHER READING

The emergence of a north–south divide in British voting is discussed in *A Nation Dividing? The Electoral Map of Great Britain, 1979–1987* by Ron Johnston et al. (Longmans, 1988) and in John Curtice and Alison Park's 'Region: New Labour, new geography?' in *Critical Elections: British Parties and Voters in Long-Term Perspective* (Sage, 1999). The story is brought up to date in 'The election results in the UK regions' in *Britain Votes 2005* by Ron Johnston et al. (Oxford University Press, 2005) and 'The British general election of 2010: a three-party contest or three two-party contests?' by Ron Johnston and Charles Pattie (*The Geographical Journal*, 2011).

—CHAPTER 23—

Taxpayers of Surrey Heath unite: identifying the most left-wing and right-wing constituencies

Chris Hanretty

No reader of the present volume will be astonished by the claim that Glasgow North East and Surrey Heath are two very different parliamentary constituencies. They differ socially and culturally in very many ways. Yet there is something peculiarly political which makes these two constituencies special. That is their opinion on one of the major dividing lines between left and right: taxation.

For some years, the British Election Study (BES) has asked people to place their views on taxation on a scale from zero to ten, where zero indicates that government should *cut* taxes a lot and spend much less on health and social services, and ten indicates that governments should *raise* taxes a lot and spend much more on health and social services. Across Great Britain, the average response is slightly above six, indicating a (modest) preference for more tax and spend. The great size and reach of the BES means we can be fairly confident that this average – drawn from the responses of 16,000 people up and down the country – is a fair reflection of the public mood overall.

But MPs are not elected by the nation as a whole, but by the smaller set of voters resident in their constituencies. So while this overall figure is useful, many politicians would much rather know the views in their particular neck of the woods. This is harder to gauge using standard surveys, because only a few residents of each Parliamentary seat are surveyed, too few to say much about their views with any confidence.

We need to give the standard survey data a helping hand. To do this, we can exploit the fact that opinion about big, nationally divisive issues like taxation is fairly predictable: women, renters, public sector workers, and those in social groups C2 and DE tend to support taxation more than everyone else. With information on just seven characteristics (gender, accommodation type, marital status, private/public sector, age group, educational qualifications, and social grade), coupled with information on the constituency you live in, we can arrive at a pretty good estimate of how opinion looks for a large number of particular *types* of people.

To move from opinion across types of people to opinion across constituencies, we need to exploit a second source of information. The census includes some basic information on every single resident of the country, and we can use this to identify how many voters of each type live in a constituency. Combining the likely opinion of each voter 'type', we can produce an estimate of the views each MP's voters hold about the big issues of the day. This takes us back to Glasgow North East and Surrey Heath. Using this method, we find that these two seats are at opposite ends of the country in more than one respect. The voters of Glasgow North East represent one end of the spectrum of constituency opinion on tax and spend, while the residents of Surrey Heath form the other pole.

The figure shows the top and bottom five constituencies, alongside an estimate of their position, and a line indicating a measure of uncertainty around the estimate (what is known as the margin of error). On a ten-point scale, the average resident of Glasgow North East places themselves nearly three-quarters of a point more in favour of more tax and spending than the average voter in the nation as a whole. Down in Surrey Heath the average voter is three-fifths of a point lower than the national average, reflecting a greater enthusiasm for spending and tax cuts. Differences of less than a point might not sound a lot – but it's the same size of effect that you would get if you changed every private sector worker in the constituency into a public sector worker, or vice versa.

CONSTITUENCIES WITH THE HIGHEST AND LOWEST SUPPORT FOR HIGHER TAX AND GREATER PUBLIC SPENDING

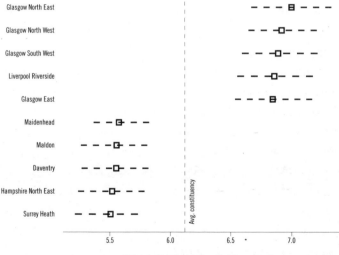

Higher values indicate greater support for taxing and spending

This method can be easily extended to produce estimates for any question of interest. For example, the BES also asked a similar question about crime – where numbers closer to zero indicate that the respondent thought it more important to reduce crime than protect the rights of the accused, and numbers closer to ten the reverse. The average across the UK was 3.35, and opinion on crime is much less different across constituencies than opinion on taxation which means that the probabilities of each of the listed constituencies being most extreme are all very small. Still, the five constituencies where highest priority would be given to reducing crime were Leicester East (an estimated average of 2.87), Boston and Skegness (2.89), South Holland and The Deepings (2.90) Makerfield (2.90) and Aldridge-Brownhills (2.92). By contrast, the rights of aspiring graffiti artists are more likely to be upheld in Bristol West (4.41), Vauxhall (4.46), Lewisham Deptford (4.50), Dulwich and West Norwood (4.51) and Streatham (4.52).

This isn't just an exercise in measurement – and it's more than confirming what we (think we) already know. Knowing about constituency opinion matters because MPs often claim to reflect the views of their constituents. Research looking into the link between what constituencies think and what MPs do has been hampered by the fact that it's very difficult to get good measurements of constituency opinion. The limited research that exists has had to rely on proxies for opinion. Sometimes, this gets really crude – as when researchers assume that heavily Catholic constituencies will favour abortion restrictions. By providing better measures, we not only get a better map of the political lie of the land, we also make it possible to test some fundamental claims about representation in the UK.

FURTHER READING

For details of the particular technique discussed, see 'Bayesian multilevel estimation with poststratification: state-level estimates from national polls' by David K Park et al. (*Political Analysis*, 2004), though note this is not for the statistically faint-hearted. For previous research on the link between constituency opinion and MPs' behaviour, particularly in free votes, see John Baughman's 'Party, constituency, and representation: Votes on abortion in the British House of Commons' (*Public Choice*, 2004) and 'Accounting for the Voting Patterns of British MPs on Free Votes' by John Hibbing et al. (*Legislative Studies Quarterly*, 1987). This chapter is based on ESRC-funded research (Grant number ES/K003666/1) by Nick Vivyan and Chris Hanretty. More information about the method can be found at the project website www.constituencyopinion.org.uk.

CHAPTER 24

National trends and regional variation: local elections

Colin Rallings

The national media tends to treat the annual round of local elections as little more than a staging post en route to what they regard as 'the real thing': the general election. Up to a point they are right. The political parties themselves are careful to manage expectations, but nonetheless set targets and benchmarks against which they claim their performance and that of their opponents should be judged. Poor local election results can throw parties into turmoil and trigger leadership challenges. Significant seat gains often provide important campaigning momentum. Yet each year local elections throw up what a 2013 *Guardian* editorial called 'a muddling mosaic of local votes' which reflect two underlying patterns of behaviour.

First, it is clear that British voters are increasingly willing to pick horses for courses when casting votes. This includes supporting different parties at different elections held at the same time (in 1997 up to one in five voters chose to vary their support at the coincident general and local elections; at the 2009 local and European

Parliament elections the level of so-called 'split ticket' voting was even higher) or simply deciding to turn out for some elections but not bother at others. It is little surprise therefore that opinion polls asking respondents how they will vote at the next general election tend to provide only modest guidance to local election outcomes.

Labour, for example, always struggles to get its would-be supporters to the ballot box. Over a period of twenty years its standing in the polls has always been higher than the actual vote it secures at either the annual local contests in May or, in most cases, even at general elections. In 2014 Labour's national equivalent vote at the local elections was just 31 per cent compared with an average opinion poll rating of 35 per cent over the previous month.

The Liberal Democrats, by contrast, usually outperform their poll ratings. In part, at least until they joined the coalition in 2010, this was assisted by being a convenient home for anti-government protest. However, it also reflects a long-standing policy of building from the bottom up, spreading from ward to constituency through intensive local election campaigning.

In doing so, they often retain the local votes of people who would never dream of supporting them at a general election. In 2010 the Liberal Democrat general election vote in Watford amounted to just three-quarters of that at the coincident local election. The party failed to win the parliamentary constituency but the Lib Dem mayor was easily re-elected. She won again in 2014 in the midst of her party's electoral meltdown, with the Lib Dem local vote also holding up in well-established strongholds like Cheltenham, Eastleigh and South Lakeland.

The match between the Conservatives' opinion poll scores and local election performance has historically tended to be much closer. However it is noticeable that their local vote share has been disproportionately affected by the rise of UKIP and the possible loss of some of their older supporters, those most likely to turn out at elections of all kinds. In both 2013 and 2014 the Conservatives were adrift of an average opinion poll score in the low thirties. It remains to be seen whether these sometime UKIP supporters will return to the Conservatives at the general election.

UKIP itself has taken a similar approach to the Liberal Democrats in trying to mitigate the adverse effects of the first-past-the-post electoral system at local level. Although its share of seats in the 2013 and 2014 local elections fell far short of its share of the vote, it has begun to build a councillor base in parts of eastern England and the midlands in particular, from which it will now draw its general election targets.

Such variations in party support highlight a second aspect of local election behaviour. Local personalities, local issues, and the record of councils can and do count.

Whichever party is in office locally can suffer the same kind of anti-incumbent reaction as its counterpart at Westminster. This tends not so much to be related to levels of local taxation as to the provision of services, or perceived lack of it. The impact is all the more powerful if accompanied by a local media campaign. Planning issues such as the siting of supermarkets and trivial if highly salient matters such as car parking charges have resulted in local swings against the national trend.

For example, in 2003 Labour gained Plymouth directly from the Conservatives despite losing some 800 seats and control of thirty councils nationwide. The key issue for many local voters was opposition to a proposal to close two care homes.

Equally, voters sometimes express approval of their local council by backing it contrary to the national swing. The most famous example dates back to 1990 when Conservative victories in the low poll tax London boroughs of Wandsworth and Westminster were used by the party to deflect attention from the drubbing it had received elsewhere. In 2014 the Liberal Democrats made gains in their flagship London borough of Sutton at the same time as losing control to the Conservatives in neighbouring Kingston-upon-Thames for the first time in two decades.

It is also the case that individual incumbent councillors tend to perform better than their party and that the 'personal vote' they attract among ward electors can allow them to survive an adverse national swing. Surveys suggest they campaign harder than most of their opponents too, a trait also shared by most Liberal Democrat candidates, and now most UKIP candidates too.

Nor have independents and small groups been eliminated from local government. On general election day in 2005 the candidate from the wonderfully named 'Idle Toad' party easily defeated Labour and Conservative opponents in South Ribble, Lancashire; in two wards in Stockton-on-Tees the Ingleby Barwick Independent Society polled more votes than all three major parties put together at the *local* contest.

Local elections do provide a useful guide to the ebb and flow of political fortunes. But they are more than simply national events played out on the local stage. At least in part their overall outcome will always be the product of countervailing results in different local authorities across the country. But they can be key in allowing insurgent parties to grow support at a local level as a base for national campaigns in the same area.

FURTHER READING

The standard work on local elections is Colin Rallings and Michael Thrasher's *Local Elections in Britain* (Routledge, 1997) – now in urgent need of updating. Detailed results for every local election since 1985 are published in the *Local Elections Handbook* series (Elections Centre, Plymouth University, annually). Voters choosing different parties at coincident elections are discussed by Colin Rallings and Michael Thrasher in 'Another (small) step on the road towards a multi-party Britain: turnout and party choice at the 2009 local and European Parliament elections' (*British Politics*, 2009), and the role of local elections in building a constituency base is discussed in 'Local Elections as a "Stepping Stone": Does Winning Council Seats Boost the Liberal Democrats' Performance in General Elections?' by David Cutts (*Political Studies*, 2014).

—CHAPTER 25—

Malapportionment and gerrymandering, UK-style: electoral bias

David Rossiter

In 2010 the Conservatives won 36.1 per cent of the votes at the general election, in return for which 306 Conservative MPs were elected, twenty short of the number needed for a majority. Five years earlier, Labour won 35.2 per cent but got 356 MPs, a clear sixty-seat majority in the Commons with a lower vote share than that which left the Conservatives twenty seats short. Everyone knows that Britain's simple plurality – or first-past-the-post – electoral system discriminates against smaller parties. But it is less well understood why, and how, it is currently biased against the Conservatives.

One simple way to measure the extent of electoral bias is to create a 'notional election result' – the probable Westminster outcome if the two parties obtained equal vote shares nationally. Under an unbiased system, equal votes would translate to equal seats. But in 1997, when the Conservatives and Labour together won 74 per cent of the votes, if each had received 37 per cent – distributed across the 650 constituencies in the same relative proportions as the actual result – Labour would have had eighty-two more MPs than the Conservatives. The next two election results were even more biased: an equal split of votes would have produced a Labour lead of 142 seats in 2001 and 112 in 2005. And in 2010, with equal shares of their joint 65 per cent of the votes, Labour would have had a 54-seat lead over the Conservatives.

British constituencies are defined by non-partisan Boundary Commissions so why do such biased election outcomes occur? Their existence lies in two common US electoral practices: malapportionment and gerrymandering. Neither is deliberately deployed in the UK, but their functional equivalents are built in to the system.

Malapportionment occurs when parties benefit from their support being concentrated in constituencies with smaller electorates. The table shows ten imaginary constituencies – A, B, C, etc. – under three different scenarios. Scenario one indicates the effect of malapportionment in a contest between two parties, X and Y, who share 5,000 votes equally. Party X's votes are concentrated in the smaller constituencies – those with 300 and 500 votes in total. It wins seven seats (marked in bold in the table) to Y's three, despite the two parties each having 2,500 votes overall.

ELECTORAL BIAS: THREE SCENARIOS

	A	B	C	D	E	F	G	H	I	J	TOTAL
SCENARIO ONE: MALAPPORTIONMENT											
Total	300	300	300	500	500	500	500	700	700	700	5,000
X	**200**	**200**	**200**	**300**	**300**	**300**	**400**	200	200	200	2,500
Y	100	100	100	200	200	200	100	**500**	**500**	**500**	2,500

	A	B	C	D	E	F	G	H	I	J	TOTAL
SCENARIO TWO: MALAPPORTIONMENT THROUGH ABSTENTION											
Total	500	500	500	500	500	500	500	500	500	500	5,000
Abstain	200	200	150	150	100	100	100	100	50	50	1,200
X	**250**	**250**	**200**	**250**	**250**	**250**	**250**	150	50	50	1,900
Y	50	50	150	150	150	150	150	**250**	**400**	**400**	1,900
SCENARIO THREE: DIFFERENT VOTE EFFICIENCY											
Total	500	500	500	500	500	500	500	500	500	500	5,000
X	**290**	**290**	**270**	**270**	**280**	**280**	**270**	**270**	140	140	2,500
Y	210	210	230	230	220	220	230	230	**360**	**360**	2,500

This type of malapportionment is a big problem in the UK. In 1997, for example, the average electorates in seats won by Labour and Conservative were 67,544 and 72,137 respectively. This partly resulted from national variations: in Wales (where Labour is by far the stronger) the average constituency had 55,015 voters compared to England's 68,927; Scotland's average then was 54,806 but thirteen MPs were lost after devolution and in 2010 it was 65,383 compared to England's 78,189. Malapportionment also results from where the parties' seats are: many urban constituencies (again where Labour is strong) grow slower, or even decline in size, between boundary reviews while suburban and rural ones (where the Conservatives are stronger) grow more quickly. The result is that when successive elections are held using the same constituencies the gap between the two parties' average electorates widens, to Labour's advantage.

A similar problem operates when one party's votes are concentrated where turnout is lowest. In the table's second scenario all constituencies have 500 voters, but abstentions range from 50 to 200. The two parties share the 3,800 votes cast but X's are concentrated where turnout is lower and it wins seven seats. Again, this is a problem in the UK: in 2010, for example, turnout averaged 61 per cent in Labour-won seats but 68 per cent in Conservative-won seats.

What about 'gerrymandering', the practice of drawing constituency boundaries to favour one party? This may not happen deliberately in the UK but can result by default if one party's votes are more efficiently distributed than another's. A party's votes in each constituency can be divided into three types: *wasted votes* (cast in seats where it loses); *effective* (needed to get the party into first place); and *surplus* (extra votes over and above those needed to win).

A party benefits if its votes are more effectively distributed than its opponents' – if it 'wins small but loses large'. The table's third scenario shows two equally popular parties in ten seats of equal size, with no abstentions; because X's votes are more efficiently distributed it wins eight seats to Y's 2. Of X's 2,500 votes, 71.5 per cent are effective, compared to just 11.3 per cent of Y's.

Given the geographies of different parties' support, there are some (mainly urban) areas where Labour wins all of the seats with little more than 40 per cent of the votes, whereas in others (mainly in rural England) the same happens for the Conservatives. Elsewhere a small shift in vote shares can mean one party losing all of the seats to its opponent (as with the two Swindon constituencies in 2010); when that happens widely, one party benefits most. In 1997, 2001 and 2005 – assisted by anti-Conservative tactical voting – Labour won narrow victories all over the country. As a result, the Conservatives lost really big, with millions of wasted votes.

In practice, all three types of bias operate simultaneously, but it is possible to isolate their effects. In 2001, the total pro-Labour bias was 142 seats; twenty of those were due to constituency size variations, thirty-eight to turnout variations and seventy-four to Labour's more efficient distribution, with the remainder due to other, minor, causes. The total bias fell to fifty-four in Labour's favour in 2010, eighteen of those seats because of variations in size and thirty-one in turnout; there was no efficiency benefit for either party then.

The large bias against their party explains why Conservatives were so eager to reform constituency boundaries after 2010. In addition to reducing the number of MPs from 650 to 600, in 2011 the coalition legislated to require almost all UK constituencies to have electorates within +/-5 per cent around a national average – with redistributions every five years. Although this would have only dealt with one source of bias, it would still have helped the Conservatives considerably. Estimates suggest that if the 600 new constituencies the Boundary Commissions were minded to recommend in 2013 had been used in 2010, the size bias would have been totally removed and the Conservative lead over Labour (306:258 in a 650-MP House) extended to 302:223. Some pro-Labour bias would have remained, but it would have been just sixteen seats rather than fifty-four. But the defeat of House of Lords reform led to the Liberal Democrats vetoing the boundary changes, meaning that the Conservatives still face an uphill battle in 2015.

FURTHER READING

The fullest account of the methodology for assessing bias, applied to the UK, is *From Votes to Seats: the Operation of the UK Electoral System since 1945* by Ron Johnston et al. (Manchester University Press, 2001). These analyses have been updated for every subsequent election – see Ron Johnston and Charles Pattie's 'The British General Election of 2010: a Three-Party Contest or Three Two-Party Contests?' (*The Geographical Journal*, 2011). On the probable outcome of the prematurely terminated Boundary Commission redistribution aimed at removing the size bias before the 2015 general election, see Ron Johnston's 'Which Map? Which Government? Malapportionment and Gerrymandering UK Style' (*Government and Opposition*, 2014).

CHAPTER 26

We know where you live: the importance of local candidates

Jocelyn Evans

When you vote in an election, do you care where the candidates live? Election candidates go out of their way to stress their local connections – however tenuous they may be in some cases – and residence is certainly one measure of localness.

Evidence from other political systems has long revealed an effect based on how local the candidates are. In the '70s and '80s, this was tested in different settings – from New Zealand local elections, to US gubernatorial elections, even US presidential elections with the so-called 'home-state advantage'. Britain, however, was largely overlooked. As the Irish geographer, Anthony Parker, put it, Britain 'often yield[s] unknown and inaccessible public representatives, who are often voted for merely because they are standing for a particular political party'.

But if that's true, why do election candidates go to such efforts to tell you how local they are? A renewed interest in the localism of British candidates has accompanied the reinvigoration of regional and local politics, and the decline of deferential party support. Recent research has been able to test this in two different ways, and both confirm that voters are indeed influenced by how far candidates live from them.

The first approach is to run survey experiments on the electorate. Presenting profiles for two fictional Parliamentary candidates, these studies ask people to compare candidates on different attributes, such as approachability and effectiveness, as well as the likelihood of voting for them, while the profile of one candidate is changed by age, gender, occupation, education and the like. Unbeknownst to respondents, these attributes are randomly varied, which enables the researchers to test how changing these factors influences voters' views of the candidates. Such experiments have managed to dispel some popular misconceptions about candidate preferences, such as voters preferring male to female candidates. But one of the strongest effects comes from comparing a candidate who lives locally to one who lives a substantial distance away – voters overwhelmingly score the local candidate higher across all attributes. Making one of the fictitious candidates live 120 miles away from a constituency, as opposed to living within the seat, was enough to generate a 15 percentage point swing away from that candidate.

The second approach, which has now been used in both British and Irish elections, is to test the effect in the field: mapping where voters and candidates live, measuring the distance between them, and then looking for any differences in the likelihood of voting for a candidate. Identifying where candidates and voters live is simple. For any British election, candidate addresses are published in the Statement of Persons Nominated – the list of candidates released with the Notice of Poll before the election. The British Election Study provides a sample of the electorate, including a relatively precise residential location (anonymously, of course). Looking at a sample of 146 English constituencies in the 2010 general election, and taking into account the usual predictors of vote – the voter's partisanship, which candidate if any is incumbent, the socio-economic condition of the area, and so on – the results were clear: whatever the voter's initial preferences, they were on average more likely to support a candidate who lived nearby than one who lived further away.

The table shows how large this effect was. The top two lines show the real outcomes – how far on average a Conservative, Liberal Democrat and Labour candidate lived from their constituents, and the average share of the vote they won in the 146 constituencies examined. The 'Same' row estimates what would happen if all the candidates lived the same distance away (26 km, the average across all candidates), then the three successive scenarios put the candidates one by one at a hefty 120 km away. For the Conservative, this would result in more than a 15 percentage point drop on their real average share. For Liberal Democrat and Labour candidates, who have smaller average shares to start, there is still a reduction of nearly ten points. To put this in context, a reduction of just eight points for the winning candidate, with half of that going to the runner up, would be enough to change the result in one-third of these 146 constituencies.

Distance mattered.

VOTES FOR PARTY CANDIDATES AS DISTANCE BETWEEN CANDIDATE ADDRESS AND VOTER ADDRESS CHANGES (%)

	CONSERVATIVE	LIBERAL DEMOCRAT	LABOUR
Distance (km)	25.42	29.46	19.27
Real	53.40	24.57	22.03
Same	53.52	25.31	21.17
Far Tory	**37.62**	33.97	28.40
Far LD	60.86	**15.08**	24.07
Far Labour	59.52	28.15	**12.33**

These findings don't mean that parties and candidates should start including Zoopla in their campaign toolkit. In the end, the location of candidates is often out of the parties' control, and indeed visible parachuting of formerly 'foreign' candidates into new homes in alien constituencies can backfire spectacularly. But it does demonstrate the importance that voters attach to local presence, an attribute often belittled in Britain in the past, and still underestimated by many commentators.

We still don't know for sure exactly *why* voters like local candidates. Is it that they think a local candidate is more likely to have an investment in their area? Or that a local candidate will be more accessible? Or just that a local candidate is 'one of us'? But we can be sure that the effect exists. Local connections are often seen as vital for local government (incidentally, the distance test works there too). We should recognise that the same applies more than we thought to our Westminster representatives.

FURTHER READING

The survey experiments can be found in Rosie Campbell and Philip Cowley's 'What voters want: reactions to candidate characteristics in a survey experiment' (*Political Studies*, 2013). The 2010 general election test is reported in Kai Arzheimer and Jocelyn Evans's 'Geolocation and voting: Candidate-voter distance effects on party choice in the 2010 UK general election in England' (*Political Geography*, 2012). For a similar approach in the Republic of Ireland, read Maciej Gorecki and Michael Marsh's 'Not just "friends and neighbours": canvassing, geographic proximity and voter choice' (*European Journal of Political Research*, 2012).

'Winning here!'

CAMPAIGN SLOGAN USED BY THE LIBERAL DEMOCRATS, TO
EMPHASISE THEIR LOCAL SUCCESS (USED LESS THESE DAYS)

CHAPTER 27

Looking good for election day: do attractive candidates do better?

Caitlin Milazzo

W e use first impressions every day to judge the people we encounter. Often based largely or solely on someone's appearance, these snap judgements help us to determine who we consider competent or trustworthy. As a result, first impressions tend to predict a wide range of behaviours. Attractiveness, in particular, is a powerful attribute. Teachers who are perceived to be more attractive receive more positive student evaluations, even when the teachers are evaluated using only short video clips with no sound. Similarly, attractive university professors tend to receive evaluations that are, on average, nearly a point higher on a five-point scale. Attractive individuals are more likely to receive assistance from strangers, and attractive children tend to receive more attention from adults. Attractiveness also conveys a variety of benefits in business: individuals who are perceived to be attractive are more likely to be hired and promoted, and they tend to receive higher incomes.

Such superficial judgements should, of course, play no role in politics. Except that there is considerable evidence that they do. In a famous study from the United States, Todorov and his colleagues showed that US congressional candidates who were judged more competent in the laboratory (based on as little as thirty-three milliseconds of exposure to photos) were the real election winners about 70 per cent of the time. The effect of appearance is by no means limited to the US; studies document the relationship between appearance and election results in countries around the world. Indeed, the effect of appearance is so significant that one recent study was able to predict French election results using the judgements that Swiss children made from looking at photos of the candidates.

There are many things we might infer about political candidates based on their appearance. Do they appear to be competent? Do they appear to be honest or caring? All of these are traits that people value in their political leaders. However, unlike these traits, attractiveness conveys no meaningful information about a candidate's ability to represent his or her constituents. And yet studies document a relationship between perceptions of attractiveness and electoral success in Australia, Brazil, Canada, Finland, Germany, Mexico and Switzerland. British elections are no exception. Attractiveness has been shown to give an edge in races where the candidates were members of the opposite sex. Women, in particular, are more likely to prefer an attractive candidate. Attractiveness is also a predictor of success in local elections where voters tend to care less about the outcome.

One recent study of the 2010 British general election asked undergraduates from an American university to evaluate real British candidates using quickly formed first impressions of a photograph of the candidate's face. To minimise the differences between the photographs, all 150 photographs featured candidates facing forward, all the photographs and faces were roughly the same size and resolution, and all the candidates were smiling. The photographs were paired according to actual electoral races in which the candidates ran against each other. The students were shown two images for each election, of the winner and the second place candidate, with each picture being shown one at a time for less than one second each. Participants had thirty seconds to decide which candidate they thought was the more attractive of the pair.

There were many races where the students had a clear preference on which candidate was more attractive. Conservative candidates were rated as being more attractive 58 per cent of the time, compared with 41 per cent for Labour candidates and 49 per cent for Liberal Democrat candidates. In addition, students were less likely to find incumbent MPs attractive. These differences may be due to the age of the candidates, as the incumbents tend to be older than the challengers, and in general the study did find that students tended to rate younger candidates as being more attractive; candidates younger than forty years old were, on average, rated as being the more attractive of the pair by 59 per cent of participants, while the percentage dropped to 34 per cent for candidates older than sixty. This is perhaps unsurprising given that the average age of the students was only twenty years.

More surprisingly, however, these perceptions of attractiveness predicted 58 per cent of these election contests. And in close races – those decided by less than 5 per cent of the votes – attractiveness successfully predicted the outcomes of almost three-quarters (72 per cent) of the elections. Remember that this was using only American students' judgements about the candidates' attractiveness, so the accuracy of this prediction is particularly surprising, as they were unlikely to know anything else about the politicians they were rating.

What exactly is the payoff of being deemed the more attractive candidate? To find this out, the authors calculated the difference in the percentage of votes received by a candidate who was rated as being attractive by 25 per cent of students versus a candidate who is rated as being more attractive by 75 per cent of the students. They found that the more attractive candidate was predicted to have more than a 2 percentage point advantage over their less attractive opponent, even after taking into account the candidate's party and their party's vote share in the constituency in the previous election, as well as the candidate's campaign spending, gender, age, and whether they were an incumbent MP. In the grand scheme of things, 2 percentage points might not seem like much. But consider that approximately thirty constituencies were decided by less than 2 per cent of votes in 2010, and also that the Conservative Party needed just twenty additional seats to gain a majority in parliament. All of a sudden a difference of 2 percentage points does not seem so small.

FURTHER READING

More information about the findings and the study presented here can be found in Kyle Mattes and Caitlin Milazzo's 'Pretty Faces, Marginal Races: Predicting Election Outcomes Using Positive and Negative Trait Assessments of British Parliamentary Candidate Images' (*Electoral Studies*, 2014). The methodology used in this study was first developed by Alexander Todorov et al. – see 'Inferences of Competence from Faces Predict Election Outcomes' (*Science*, 2005) – who used rapidly determined first impressions of candidate competence to explain US Congressional outcomes. For information on the role of first impressions, see 'Very First Impressions' by Moshe Bar et al. (*Emotion*, 2006) and Ingrid R. Olson and Christy Marshuetz's 'Facial Attractiveness is Appraised in a Glance' (*Emotion*, 2005). There are also a number of other interesting studies about the role of candidate traits in British elections, including 'Ballot Photographs as Cues in Low-Information Elections' by Susan Banducci et al. (*Political Psychology*, 2008), and a series of papers by Mark Shephard and Rob Johns, including their 'Facing the Voters: The Potential Impact of Ballot Paper Photographs' (*Political Studies*, 2011).

CHAPTER 28

What's in a name: ballot order effects

Galina Borisyuk

Those wishing to seek elected office in the UK may need to change their surname. Other things being equal, it is better to be Brown not Smith. But Brown and Smith are each better than Borisyuk – not that I'm thinking of standing.

If you study the distribution of votes cast in local council wards where voters are selecting more than a single councillor, you will notice a high level of unused votes. Say 1,000 electors each have three votes the total number of votes cast could be 3,000; but it often isn't. Some unused votes arise because parties fail to field enough candidates for the number of seats available; three seats but only two candidates, for example. In such cases the more partisan electors might baulk at the idea of using their spare vote for a rival party and would not use their full quota. But even in those elections where the parties field full slates of candidates you still find some voters (about one in fifteen in London and as high as one in nine in other larger cities) who do not take full advantage of all the votes available to them.

Maybe these unused votes arise because people did not understand the voting system. Since most people read text (in this case a ballot paper) from left to right and from top to bottom, you might think that candidates located towards the top of the ballot paper should do better than those located towards the bottom. After examining tens of thousands of local ballots one study discovered that a candidate's finishing position within a party slate depends upon the position on the ballot paper as a whole, his or her alphabetic rank within the party slate, and whether they were an incumbent seeking re-election or challenging an incumbent. To be fair, incumbency mattered more than alphabetic order but surnames were associated with vote differences. The alphabetic advantage between the first and last placed candidates on the ballot paper was real, and increased along with the number of available seats and the number of competitors.

Alphabetic bias is not restricted to these relatively complex ballots. It appears to extend to very simple electoral contests. Alphabetic effects have been found even in single-member local council seats. In the simplest possible electoral situation – that is, two candidates contesting 1 seat – there is a mean difference of eleven votes (or 0.6 percentage points) between the person placed second and bottom of the ballot paper compared to the name encountered first on the ballot paper. As the number of candidates increases so the difference in vote between first and last in the alphabetic order also grows.

What are the consequences of this for representative government? A separate study examined over 600,000 candidate names that appeared on local council election ballots from the early '70s onwards. They were divided into ten equal categories according to surname. It turns out that the distribution among those elected is clustered towards the first three surname categories (A'Beckett to Flello in this case). The elected are under-represented in the bottom five categories (surnames running from Kennedy to Zygadllo).

This evidence suggests that approximately 2,050 councillors elected between 1973 and 2012 owe their election to ballot position alone. This might not seem like a large number over a long period although for the 2,050 that were not elected because their name happened to be further down the ballot paper it must hurt.

But there was something else in the data. The relationship between surname and electoral support is not entirely linear. The advantage for those at the very top of the ballot was not as high as expected. One possibility was an association between alphabetic order and ethnicity. Non-European names, for example, are particularly abundant in the first surname category. In order to examine this ethnic dimension computer software was used to allocate surnames into three types: British (Anglo Saxon, Celtic), other European and non-European. It became clear that in addition to relative ballot position a candidate's vote was also being affected – positively or negatively – by perceived ethnic origin.

There are two ways of addressing this issue using the same election results as before. First, in the case of wards that elect multiple councillors comparisons can be made among candidates standing for the same party. Other things being equal, over this forty year period candidates with British surnames perform best while non-European candidates performed worst. Between 1,422 and 7,150 seats could have been won by a different person had the names on the ballot papers been configured differently.

Second, the analysis of 70,000 single-member seats considered the patterns of candidate recruitment, or ethnic transition, across electoral cycles. This showed that party vote is adversely affected when British candidates are replaced by those with European and non-European surnames while the opposite pattern of succession is associated with a boost in vote. The effect of this? Up to 5,167 of these single-member seats (7 per cent of the total) were won/lost by parties by margins that might be explained by such ethnic transitions.

What is to be done?

We could do nothing, of course, and allow parties to seek out and recruit candidates with appropriate surnames in a frantic 'name race'. Political careerists should download the deed poll forms immediately. Another solution is to follow practice elsewhere. Australia and the United States are two countries where ballot order is randomised. This would be fairly cheap to implement although it makes hand-counting of ballots more complicated. A third approach might be to reform local elections and abolish the practice of multiple seats. Some voters are clearly perplexed by a complex ballot but imagine how perplexed these voters are by other voting systems now widely employed across the UK.

None of these solutions address the issue of name discrimination, however. Local parties are trying very hard to recruit candidates from under-represented groups. But we should acknowledge that currently there are some voters who are still reluctant to support candidates with 'unusual' surnames.

FURTHER READING

For an examination about unused votes the best source is 'Unused votes in English Local Government Elections: Effects and Explanations' by Colin Rallings et al. (*Journal of Elections, Public Opinion and Parties*, 2009), while a more detailed analysis about the electoral effects of ballot ordering can be found in 'Ballot Order Positional Effects in British Local Elections, 1973–2011' by Richard Webber et al. (*Parliamentary Affairs*, 2013). The extent of name discrimination is investigated in 'Candidate Ethnic Origins and Voter Preferences: Examining Voting Bias in Local Elections in Britain' by Michael Thrasher et al. (a paper presented at the 71st Midwest Political Science Association conference, 2013).

—CHAPTER 29—

The lady's not for spurning: the electorate and women candidates

Elizabeth Evans

Women make up 51 per cent of the population, but just 22 per cent of MPs in the House of Commons. The Prime Minister has described this as 'scandalous'; Ed Miliband thinks it a 'crisis of representation'.

There are multiple possible explanations for this under-representation, but perhaps the two most popular are that the electorate are biased against women candidates and that there aren't enough women who want to stand for election. There is no evidence to support the first of these claims, and the second claim is only partially true.

Some research in the US has shown that women tend to prefer a female candidate (62 per cent) while most men prefer a male candidate (68 per cent), and US political scientists have found a 10 percentage point difference between black women's and white men's probability of voting for a black female candidate.

But in the UK, although recent research has found that people may perceive female and male candidates differently – women tend to be seen as more approachable, men more experienced – this does not translate into an overall electoral advantage for either sex.

At the last general election in 2010, in seats where Labour experienced a drop in vote share (which was the overwhelming majority of seats) the percentage fall was almost identical regardless of the sex of the candidate (-7.4 points for women, -7.3 for men). There was similarly no difference in the performance of female and male candidates standing on behalf of either the Conservatives or Liberal Democrats. And while there have been occasional revolts against the use of mechanisms such as all-women shortlists – as in Blaenau Gwent in 2005, where Labour lost a rock-solid seat after the imposition of a woman candidate from outside the constituency – such events are the exceptions not the rule; in general studies have found no electoral penalty to women selected on all-women shortlists.

In understanding why there are not more women MPs we can therefore rule out bias on the part of the electorate.

The table shows the percentage of candidates and MPs who were female between 1979 and 2010.

It illustrates two key points: 1) the percentage of female candidates and MPs has increased (albeit at a relatively slow pace); but 2) despite this progress the percentage of male candidates remains significantly higher than the percentage of female candidates.

At the last election there were almost four times as many male candidates as female. Women made up just 21 per cent of candidates, resulting in 22 per cent of MPs; yet more evidence that the problem is not the voters.

PERCENTAGE OF FEMALE CANDIDATES AND MPS 1979–2010

ELECTION	FEMALE CANDIDATES	FEMALE MPS
1979	8	3
1983	11	4
1987	14	6
1992	19	9
1997	18	18
2001	19	18
2005	20	20
2010	21	22

A large part of the problem is that political parties are disproportionately male – and it is from political parties that candidates are
drawn. While it's difficult to get accurate and agreed figures of party
membership, one estimate from 2009 was that women made up 39
per cent of the Conservative Party; 31 per cent of the Labour Party;
and 29 per cent of the Liberal Democrats. So, while Labour is still
aiming for equality of representation, the percentage of women in
their parliamentary party (31 per cent) is at least reflective of the
party membership. For the Conservatives and Liberal Democrats,
where women make up 16 per cent and 12 per cent of their parliamentary parties respectively, there is still some way to go.

For example, at the last election the Liberal Democrats (who
have the lowest number and percentage of women MPs) had 914
people registered on its internal list of potential parliamentary candidates; of those 262 (30 per cent) were women. This is roughly the
same proportion as in the party overall. However, when we look at

the percentage of women selected to fight the election this drops to 134 (21 per cent). In addition, it matters *which* seats women are selected for: it's no use selecting women for seats that the party has no chance of winning. To increase the overall number of women elected, parties have to ensure that women are selected in disproportionate numbers in winnable seats. That this doesn't always happen explains why 21 per cent of Lib Dem female candidates resulted in just 12 per cent of Lib Dem female MPs.

If the goal for a party is to have women make up around 50 per cent of its MPs, and 12 per cent is, in the case of the Lib Dems, the reality, we can break the 38-point difference between the goal and the reality into three components. The bulk, some twenty-one points, is the result of women not being in the party in the same proportions as men in the first place. We can then explain eight points as being the result of the party not selecting women in the same rates as men and a further nine points can be explained as a result of the party disproportionately selecting women for unwinnable seats. None of the difference can be explained as a result of women party members not putting themselves forward or by bias at the ballot box by voters.

Of course, explaining why a party has fewer women than men in its ranks is itself an interesting issue; and while there may be fewer women party members than men, there are still sufficient for the parties to select more women candidates easily enough. But this does require the party not just to select women equally but to do so disproportionately, as Labour have done with all-women shortlists. And at present there is still no evidence that they are selecting them equally.

FURTHER READING

For research into black women voters in the US see Tasha Philpot and Hanes Walton's 'One of Our Own: Black Female Candidates and the Voters Who Support Them'

(*American Journal of Political Science*, 2007). *It Takes a Candidate* by Jennifer Law-less and Richard Fox (Cambridge University Press, 2005) explores the psychological reasons why women are less likely to want to run for office. For analysis of voter reactions to candidate characteristics in the UK see Rosie Campbell and Philip Cow-ley's 'What voters want: candidate characteristics in a survey experiment' (*Political Studies*, 2013). On the Liberal Democrats and selections see Elizabeth Evans's *Gen-der and the Liberal Democrats* (Manchester University Press, 2011). Analysis of party selection methods and efforts to select more women can be found in 'Stand by your man: women's political recruitment at the 2010 general election' by Jeanette Ashe et al. (*British Politics*, 2010). Party membership figures are from Paul Whiteley 'Where have all the Members Gone?' (*Parliamentary Affairs* 2009). For the electoral impact (or lack thereof) of all-women shortlists see 'This is What Happens When You Don't Listen: All-Women Shortlists at the 2005 General Election' by David Cutts et al. (*Party Politics*, 2008).

—CHAPTER 30—

Male, pale and stale
(and likely to stay like that):
local councillors

Michael Thrasher

The stereotypical picture of local councils is that they are dominated by men the wrong side of fifty and the retired: 'male, pale
and stale', as they are often dismissed. In this case, it turns out the
stereotype is perfectly accurate: around three-quarters of local councillors are male; 96 per cent are white; and they have an average age
of fifty-eight, with more than a quarter aged over sixty-five.

Why do voters keep voting for such an unrepresentative bunch?
To answer this, imagine an election where the voters turned nasty
and voted out of office every incumbent and replaced them with rival
candidates standing in their first election. How different would the
newly elected councillors be?

The answer is: not much. The table summarises the findings from
the last four surveys of local election candidates conducted between
2010 and 2013, comparing first-time political candidates with incumbent councillors.

CHARACTERISTICS OF FIRST-TIME CANDIDATES AND INCUMBENTS (%)

	FIRST-TIME CANDIDATE	INCUMBENT
Women	32	28
Under 35 years	26	6
Over 65 years	15	27
White	95	96
University degree	56	54
Retired	22	42
Professional	51	51
Managers	27	33

It shows if every incumbent was replaced, then a few more women might be elected; the proportion of women councillors would rise from the current 28 per cent to 32 per cent. Similarly, a few more people from among minority ethnic groups might get elected but they would still be substantially under-represented – just over 5 per cent of new candidates are from minority groups, who make up 14 per cent of the population in England and Wales. Although local parties are doing better than Westminster in attracting women they are as bad or worse at recruiting ethnic minority candidates and councillors.

And would our electoral revolution breathe fresh life into local government by bringing in a wave of energetic young newcomers? To some extent. The average age of incumbent councillors is fifty-eight, but the average new challenger, at forty-eight, is no spring chicken either. Even if every incumbent was voted out, one in seven councillors would be past the age of retirement and four in ten above fifty-six years of age.

In short, little would change except that the proportion that have retired from work would reduce from around 42 per cent to around half that number. The reason voters keep voting for unrepresentative councillors in other words is because candidates are almost as unrepresentative as those they are challenging.

Candidates that are standing in their first election, just like current councillors, are typically university-educated professionals and managers. Very few are from manual occupations, a fact which appears to be missing from much of the discussion about under-representation, and given the relatively low level of remuneration available to councillors in the UK it is not surprising that it is largely the retired that have the time and commitment required to serve. Surveys of local election candidates repeatedly show that candidates receive little support from employers after they make the decision to stand and in a sizeable proportion of cases there is a hostile reaction. Some enlightened countries have sabbaticals available to elected councillors, ensuring that once they have served their communities they can resume their careers. The UK does not.

The aftermath of our hypothetical election might be more interesting: many of these new councillors would presumably be somewhat surprised to find themselves elected; sacrificing employment opportunities (not to mention the unsought strain on personal and family relationships) for the councillor's allowance would see mass resignations and a glut of by-elections.

This all paints a rather bleak picture of the current state of local government representation. With challenges like these, local councils representing a fair cross-section of the places they govern look like a distant, and forlorn, hope. We might expect, therefore, when offered an array of schemes to transform the profile of elected councillors that candidates would favour reform. Not a bit of it.

In the survey of local election candidates in 2006 two suggestions were floated: all-women shortlists and party quotas for women candidates. About one in ten candidates approved of the idea of the shortlists but a third disapproved and a further third strongly disapproved. There was a little more warmth towards party quotas but even this idea was rejected by a clear majority.

Undaunted, the following year the candidate survey tackled the idea of guaranteed seats for under-represented groups, specifically women, ethnic minorities and given the age profile of councillors, younger people. Some 87 per cent of all respondents vetoed the idea of guaranteeing council seats for women. Among women respondents the opposition to the principle fell to a mere 80 per cent. The corresponding figures for ethnic minorities and younger people are 91 per cent and 89 per cent disapproving. Clearly, although 60–75 per cent of candidates favour the recruitment of under-represented groups they are almost universally opposed to anything that smacks of affirmative action.

The following year's survey tested the proposition that if candidates were averse to quotas they might favour other methods for liberating spaces on council benches. Should councillors be forced to retire following their seventieth birthday? Or the practice of 'term limits' introduced, as used in other parts of the world, which would ensure that incumbents could only be re-elected a fixed number of times? Councillors forced to stand down by either of these measures could be offered compensation as happened to some Scottish councillors. Across the board these schemes were rejected by two in every three respondents.

Finally, when it became clear that national policy-makers were giving serious thought to using 'recall' elections as a means of curbing recalcitrant MPs, the 2013 survey floated this idea with local candidates. A clear majority, 58 per cent, supported the principle of councillors being removed from office should a quarter of the local electorate petition for that. This might be the way to transform the composition of local councils. Now, who's going to volunteer to organise a petition?

FURTHER READING

The Local Government Association, the umbrella organisation for local authorities in England and Wales, produce a bi-annual report which profiles councillors, the latest being Kelly Kettlewell and Liz Phillips's *Census of Local Authority Councillors 2013* (LGA, 2014). The annual survey of local election candidates began in 2006 and annual reports have been published; for example, *The 2009 Survey of Local Election Candidates* by Colin Rallings et al. (Improvement and Development Agency, 2009). Additionally, some academic papers utilise these survey findings, such as: 'Parties, recruitment and modernisation: Evidence from local election candidates' by Colin Rallings et al. (*Local Government Studies*, 2010) and 'BAME Candidates in Local Elections in Britain' by Michael Thrasher et al. (*Parliamentary Affairs*, 2013).

—CHAPTER 31—

The British Obamas: ethnic minority MPs

Maria Sobolewska

Before each general election, there is now a regular debate over the under-representation of visible ethnic minorities in Westminster. The main parties respond by increasing the number of minority candidates (although such increases are modest, and most still stand in unwinnable seats) and occasionally, as in 2010, the number of black and Asian MPs actually rises significantly.

According to the 2011 census, 13 per cent of British residents belong to a visible ethnic minority group. Perfect political representation would therefore require eighty-four out of 650 MPs to be of visible minority origin; today there are just twenty-seven. Yet the growth of ethnic minority representation has not spread evenly: some minority groups have a greater presence at Westminster than others; and minority MPs often have more in common with their white colleagues at Westminster than they do with the average voter from the ethnic groups they are supposed to represent.

For example, just short of 1 per cent of the population are Chinese; if Westminster represented this group equally, there would be five Chinese MPs, but in fact there are none. The black Caribbean minority, who make up almost 2 per cent of the British population, should have eleven MPs representing them, but have just one. By contrast, just over 2 per cent of the population is of recent African origin, which includes a large population of East African Indians as well as black African ethnicity. This group is well represented: out of the twenty-seven MPs representing ethnic minorities, thirteen, or nearly a half, are of African origin.

The success of black Africans is puzzling for at least two reasons. First, black African immigrants are generally less well established in the UK. Whereas Caribbean immigrants started arriving in the '50s and South Asians from the '60s and '70s (including East African Indians), black African migration started in earnest only in the '90s. Secondly, most Caribbean and South Asian immigrants had full political rights upon arrival, which includes voting in and standing for Westminster elections. Black Africans, on the other hand, are a lot more likely to hold non-Commonwealth passports and thus be excluded from British politics until they acquire British citizenship. Even among those eligible to vote, black Africans have the lowest rates of electoral registration. They are also more likely than other immigrant groups to come to this country as asylum seekers and refugees, escaping wars and persecution, making them some of Britain's most vulnerable migrants. So why have recent African immigrants and their children been so successful in elite British politics?

Since the world's most famous Western politician of recent African descent is Barack Obama, and since there is periodic speculation about who might be the 'British Obama', it is worth looking at Obama's political trajectory. He comes from a privileged background: despite some financial difficulties of his family and growing up in a single parent household (both struggles faced much more often by African Americans than white Americans), he was the son of an African immigrant who was a Harvard graduate, he went on to attend the elite university himself, both his parents were academics and he himself pursued a highly paid, high status career as a top flight law professor. In other words, apart from his skin colour and immigration background, he looked exactly like the kind of person who would end up in politics. Here the story converges with that of the UK, where we also see an increasingly uniform image of a politician. Our MPs have become steadily less diverse in terms of their social and professional background: MPs in 2010 were more likely to have prior parliamentary experience before becoming candidates (the infamous Special Advisors), have a degree and come from a professional or business background.

MOST POPULAR REASONS FOR IMMIGRATION INTO BRITAIN BY ETHNICITY (%)

	CAME TO LIVE IN BRITAIN	CAME ESCAPING WAR OR PERSECUTION	CAME FOR BETTER LIFE AND TO EARN MONEY	CAME TO JOIN FAMILY	CAME TO STUDY
Indian	6	-	48	40	19
Pakistani	2	-	30	61	13
Bangladeshi	-	-	37	51	20
Caribbean	12	-	62	26	10
African	-	20	28	22	23

*respondents were allowed to pick more than one reason
Source: Ethnic Minority British Election Study

Are Africans in the UK more likely to look like the 'right' sort of candidate to become a Westminster politician? Well yes, but as in the case of Obama, the story of privilege seems to start even before they come to the UK. Africans are not the most successful ethnic minority group in British society: they are outranked by the Indians in terms of their educational and professional success; and by

Caribbeans when it comes to social and cultural integration as measured by inter-marriage with white people. Yet, as the table shows, they are real outliers in terms of the reasons why they came to Britain. They are more likely to have been immigrants in search of a refuge from wars and conflicts, but also more likely to have come here to study, just as Obama's father once came to the US. Given the huge costs and administrative obstacles to studying in the UK, only those belonging to the African elite can make this move. Black Africans are also the least likely to come to Britain to improve their life and to earn money, as well as to join their family, which are the two most common routes of migration for everyone else. As a result, Africans are a much polarised group: globetrotting elite students at one end, penniless refugees at the other, with very little in-between.

Why does this matter? Again the example of Obama offers an interesting perspective. Since the election of the first black President of the United States, many African American voters have been disappointed. Obama did very little to address African American concerns directly and many argue that in fact things got worse for African Americans during his presidency. This highlights the dangers of assuming that an ethnic minority politician will effectively represent the group they are deemed by others to belong to.

Therefore, in the UK, if most of our ethnic minority MPs come from elite social backgrounds then in what sense can we expect them to represent the often much poorer voters from their ethnic group? Are people of minority origin who went to the same schools and universities and did the same political jobs as white MPs really more qualified to represent those who escaped wars or came to Britain to earn money, simply due to their ethnic background? In short, what difference would having a British Obama actually make?

FURTHER READING

The most recent analysis of the efforts to increase ethnic minority representation in Westminster is Maria Sobolewska's 'Party strategies, political opportunity structure and the descriptive representation of ethnic minorities in Britain' (*West European Politics*, 2013). The level of elite privilege common among the current cohort of MPs is best described in Byron Criddle's chapter 'More Diverse yet More Uniform' in *The British General Election 2010* (Palgrave Macmillan, 2010). For more information on ethnic minorities in Britain, the most recent study is analysed in great length in *The Political Integration of Ethnic Minorities in Britain* by Anthony Heath et al. (Oxford University Press, 2013).

—CHAPTER 32—

Who do we think they are: perceptions of representation

Philip Cowley

All the mainstream British political parties are – to varying degrees – now officially signed up to the principle that political institutions should broadly reflect the social characteristics of the people they represent. The idea that Anne Phillips called 'the politics of presence' – that the backgrounds of the people who represent us are at least as important as the beliefs they hold – is now a widely, if not wholly, accepted part of political discourse in the UK.

Early concern about this type of representation focused almost entirely on social class, and in particular on the lack of working-class representation. But class then fell largely off the agenda, both in 'real world' and academic debates, to be replaced, first, by sex and then, second, by ethnicity. All the main British political parties are committed to schemes aiming to raise the number of women elected as MPs (although these schemes vary in their strength and utility); there are also efforts (again, of varying strength and utility) to do something similar with the representation of ethnic minorities. Until very recently almost all senior British politicians speaking on this subject would mention both groups routinely, but with (at most) a passing reference to, usually unspecified, 'other groups'.

But do people even notice who is there? One 2009 survey, which asked people about the composition of the House of Commons, found very mixed results. In one sense, the public were not completely wrong. The House of Commons was then (and still is) overwhelmingly male, white, and middle-class – something which the public recognised. They correctly perceived that certain groups – women, gays and lesbians, the young, the disabled, Muslims – only make up a minority of parliamentarians. In these very broad terms, therefore, people get it right.

THERE ARE CURRENTLY 646 MPS IN THE WESTMINSTER PARLIAMENT – ROUGHLY WHAT PROPORTION (%) OF THEM DO YOU THINK ARE...

	MEAN ESTIMATE	ACTUAL FIGURES	DIFFERENCE
White	78	97	-19
Over 60	51	31	+20
Educated at Oxbridge	50	25	+25
From area they represent	31	46	-15
Working class	26	6	+20
Women	26	20	+6
Gay/lesbian	18	2	+16
Under 30	16	1	+15
Muslim	14	1	+13

Source: Philip Cowley 'Why not ask the audience? Understanding the public's representational priorities' (*British Politics*, 2013)

Yet some of their individual estimates were considerably out. The table shows both the average (mean) response and the real figure for nine different characteristics. At a time when there were only four Muslim MPs, for example, the public's mean estimate of 14 per cent would have meant some ninety Muslim MPs – over twenty times the actual figure. The precise number of gay and lesbian MPs might be debatable (the figure in the table is for MPs who were out and open about their sexuality, and therefore probably underestimates the total number), but the public's average estimate of 18 per cent would have represented some 116 MPs. The public also considerably over-estimated both the number of young and older MPs; the Commons suffers from much more middle-aged spread than voters think. It is also less working-class but also less Oxbridge-educated than most voters think.

The characteristic that the public got most accurate was the percentage of women. Estimates for the proportion of female MPs ranged from zero (from a not particularly perceptive respondent) to 91 per cent (ditto). But most people didn't get it as wrong: the (mean) average was 26 per cent, relatively close to the actual figure at the time, and a majority of respondents were within +/- 10 percentage points of the actual figure. There was almost no difference depending on the sex of the respondent (the mean for women was 26 per cent, the mean for men was 25 per cent).

In Nirmal Puwar's book *Space Invaders*, she talked about the 'amplification of numbers' – the idea that when previously excluded groups begin to be present in politics their very novelty will lead to perceptions of their presence being exaggerated. That may be true of some groups, and is one possible explanation for the exaggerated perceptions of Muslim and gay presence at Westminster, but it is no longer true for women MPs. Plus, as the table shows, it is also true of some groups that cannot be said to have been previously excluded: the biggest difference in the table between perception and reality comes with perceptions of the over-representation of those educated at Oxbridge.

Demonstrating voters' ignorance about matters of public policy is the political science equivalent of shooting fish in a barrel, as several other chapters in this volume indicate. But these sort of mistakes matter because they in turn drive our attitudes towards representation. The same study also asked whether respondents wanted to see more of each group in the House of Commons or not. In every case, those who wanted more of a group had a lower average estimate of existing presence than those who wanted numbers to stay as they are, and those who wanted fewer of a group had an even higher estimate. For example, those who thought women made up fewer than 15 per cent of the Commons were overwhelmingly in favour of having more women MPs: 68 per cent of this group wanted more, as opposed to just 28 per cent who wanted the numbers to stay the same. That is a net score (More minus Same) of +40. Of those who thought women made up between 15 and 40 per cent, the net score was +12. But of those who thought that women already made up 40 per cent or more of the Commons the net score fell to -14. Voters who thought there were relatively few women in Westminster wanted more while people who thought they were already present in numbers were more content with the status quo.

Another study, using the same data, found that women who wanted to see more women MPs and thought there were relatively few in the Commons already were less satisfied with democracy, and less trusting of parliament and politicians, than other women (or men).

In other words, perceptions matter. The British public may be wrong about how they see the composition of the House of Commons, but they are logical in the consequences that flow from their beliefs. How voters see their political institutions matters, even when they are wrong.

FURTHER READING

Anne Phillips's *The Politics of Presence* (Oxford University Press, 1995) has been extraordinarily influential in how this subject is discussed. The 2009 survey is reported in Philip Cowley's 'Why not ask the audience? Understanding the public's representational priorities' (*British Politics*, 2013). A study from the US which finds exactly the same relationship is Kira Sanbonmatsu's 'Gender-Related Political Knowledge and the Descriptive Representation of Women' (*Political Behavior*, 2003). The study demonstrating varying levels of political trust and satisfaction depending on perceptions of group size was Philip Cowley's 'Descriptive representation and political trust: a quasi-natural experiment utilising ignorance' (*Journal of Legislative Studies*, 2014). The 'amplification of numbers' is from Nirmal Puwar's *Space Invaders: Race, Gender and Bodies Out of Place* (Bloomsbury Academic, 2004).

—CHAPTER 33—

Attention-seeking constituents: how voters want MPs to spend their time

Nick Vivyan

Members of Parliament often talk about having two jobs. On the one hand, they engage in national policy-oriented activities: developing, debating and scrutinising policies at Westminster. On the other hand, they also engage in a great deal of constituency-oriented work, helping the voters they represent in their myriad interactions with government or throwing their weight behind local causes, such as campaigning to save a local hospital, school, or factory from closure.

Every MP has to choose how to divide their limited time and resources between their national and local responsibilities. This choice can shape their future career prospects inside Parliament, and may also shape their prospect of keeping a job in the Commons. For the rest of us, as constituents, MPs' decisions determine the type of democratic representation we get.

Look at the size of a typical MP's inbox, and it may seem that we increasingly want them to be devoted constituency servants at the expense of all else. Back in the '50s, the average MP received fewer than twenty letters per week from constituents. Now, with email and websites like theyworkforyou.com making communications easier, MPs report receiving hundreds of queries and requests per week and many say they are overwhelmed by constituency work.

This trend has sparked concern. If we all keep demanding more and more constituency work from our local MPs, and if they oblige through fear of alienating their electors, then who will be left to help make sensible laws and policies for the whole nation? Indeed, a Parliamentary committee recently looked at how MPs divide their time between Westminster work and Constituency work – and whether Parliamentary sitting hours should be adjusted in light of this.

So what do British voters really want MPs to focus their attention on? One way to learn more about this is to survey voters and ask them directly. Starting in the '70s, a number of researchers have done precisely this, providing survey respondents with a list of different MP activities or roles and asking them to pick which one they feel is the most important.

Identifying trends over time based on these studies is difficult because each tends to offer a different list of MP roles for respondents to select from. However, across studies there is a notable tendency for constituency-oriented activities to be the ones ranked most important by the British electorate. For example, in a 1979 survey almost half (45 per cent) of voters ranked MPs' constituency service activities – 'helping people in the constituency who have personal problems with the government' or 'protecting the interests of the constituency' – as the most important, while only 11 per cent ranked 'debating and voting in Parliament' as most important. More recently, a 2012 study found that over three-quarters of voters ranked constituency activities – either 'taking up and responding to issues and problems raised by constituents' or 'being active in the constituency' – as the job they most wanted their MP to do.

But while these studies tell us that British voters clearly prioritise the constituency role of their MPs, they do not tell us what *balance* of constituency and Westminster work voters expect. Do voters want an exclusive focus on constituency service, as some MPs might fear? Or do voters still recognise that their MPs needs to allocate a fair, if smaller, amount of time to their Westminster work too?

To answer these questions, a recent study asked a representative sample of just under 2,000 British voters to take part in an experiment. In this experiment – known as a 'conjoint analysis' – each respondent was given some information about two hypothetical MPs and then asked to choose which of these two MPs they would prefer to have as their local Member of Parliament.

But respondents were not all presented with the same two hypothetical MPs. Rather, the study randomly varied several of the MPs' characteristics. One of these was how each MP divided their working week between constituency work and national policy work: an MP could spend one, two, three or four days of a five-day week on constituency work, and the remaining days on national policy work. By taking MPs who spend different numbers of days on constituency work and comparing how often they were selected as the 'preferred' representative by respondents, we get a measure of what balance of work British voters want from their local MP.

The results were perhaps surprising, but also give grounds for optimism. British voters do care about how their local MP divides their time between national policy work and constituency work. The number of days per week an MP spent on constituency work had a clear effect on respondents' choices between MPs (even when they were asked to choose between a Labour and a Conservative MP). In contrast, things like the sex of the MP or their experience in Parliament – characteristics which also varied in the experiment – had little or no effect.

But voters are not as extreme in their demands for constituency work as politicians might fear. Yes, voters strongly preferred MPs who did more than the minimal amount of constituency work; that is, more than one day per week. But they also did not prefer more and more MP engagement in constituency work. In fact, voters were slightly *less* likely to choose as their preferred representative an MP who spent four days per week on constituency work than one who spent a more moderate three days per week.

Overall, the average British voter ultimately preferred their MP to spend three out of five days on constituency work and two out of five days on national policy work – in other words, a fairly moderate sixty-forty division of their time. Encouragingly, these are almost exactly the proportions of time that the new 2010 intake of MPs say they devote to these two fundamental activities. In this respect at least, the much-discussed disconnect between voters and politicians in Britain is perhaps not quite so severe after all.

FURTHER READING

The 1979 survey is reported in *The Personal Vote: Constituency Service and Electoral Independence* by Bruce Cain et al. (Harvard University Press, 1987). For the 2012 ranking survey see Rosie Campbell and Joni Lovenduski's 'Who knows what makes a good MP? Public and Parliamentarians' views compared' (*Parliamentary Affairs*, forthcoming). The experimental research is in Nick Vivyan and Markus Wagner's 'House or Home: Constituent preferences over the activities of representatives' (working paper, Durham University, 2014). Evidence on how new MPs spend time is in Matt Korris, *A Year in the Life: from member of public to Member of Parliament* (Hansard Society, 2011) and in the Procedure Committee of the House of Commons's *Sitting hours and the Parliamentary calendar* (2012).

'Public opinion is a permeating influence, and it exacts obedience to itself; it requires us to think other men's thoughts, to speak other men's words, to follow other men's habits.'

WALTER BAGEHOT, IN THE *NATIONAL REVIEW*, 1856

CHAPTER 34

A classless society: class and voting

James Tilley

In the heady days of the '90s, both the left and right in Britain claimed we were seeing the end of class politics. John Major, shortly after taking over leadership of the Conservative Party in 1990, declared he wanted to produce a 'genuinely classless society', and by 1997 John Prescott, then deputy leader of the Labour Party, claimed that in essence this aim had been met as 'we're all middle-class now'. While pronouncements by politicians are not always known for their sagacity, British electoral politics is indeed approaching a classless state. Traditionally British politics has been seen as a clash between two sides. At the party level this means one broadly on the economic left favouring redistribution and public ownership, and one broadly on the right favouring the free market and a more relaxed approach to income inequalities. At the level of the voter this means that the Labour Party attracted working-class voters and the Conservative Party middle-class voters.

The above is a caricature, but even in 1992 it was still a broadly accurate one. Measuring 'class' is not straightforward, but income and occupation are often used to get at the economic inequalities that shape behaviour and attitudes. If we look at income we see that in 1992 only 20 per cent of people in the top fifth of household incomes voted Labour, compared to more than 50 per cent in the bottom fifth of household incomes. Equally, only 26 per cent of professional and managerial workers voted Labour in 1992, compared to 50 per cent of manual workers. This all changed in 1997 and has remained changed ever since. Tony Blair famously said he wanted 'to take class out of British politics', and in a sense he did. When his government was re-elected in 2001 with another landslide victory, the gap between the top and bottom income fifths supporting Labour, which was above 30 per cent in 1992, had fallen to only 8 per cent, where it has remained.

Two questions arise from that: first, why did this change occur? Second, what implications does that have more generally for electoral change? One view is that class is no longer important because classes are simply more similar. But a better way to understand what has happened is to realise that classes are still distinctive; it is parties that have changed. Analysis of surveys collected between 1983 and today shows that differences between social groups' interests are reflected in their ideology. To put it bluntly, poor people want the state to redistribute wealth and rich people don't. Importantly, this has not changed over time. What has changed is that, under Tony Blair, the Labour Party stopped talking about redistribution and offered much more centrist economic policies. You can see this by analysing the party manifestos, in essence counting the number of phrases that support economically left-wing policies and comparing that to the number that support economically right-wing policies. Both main parties have moved to the centre over time, but the shift by Labour in the '90s is particularly pronounced. The result is that the choice on offer to voters is much less clear cut than before. People are now less likely to choose parties on the basis of their ideological beliefs (which are informed by their self-interest) because it is not clear what, if anything, separates the parties on the big ideological issues. This, in turn, leads to less socially distinctive tribes of Labour and Conservative voters.

The answer to the second question about implications is related to why this change occurred. The implications cover both changes in how voters decide between the major parties, and also whether they support those major parties at all. As the major parties have become more similar, we have seen increasing electoral volatility and an increasing vote for minor parties. We have also seen decreasing turnout which is concentrated among exactly that group whose views are now most poorly represented by the traditional parties: the working class. Poorer people have always been less likely to vote in Britain than richer people, but this difference has generally been very small. Yet at the last election in 2010 nearly 45 per cent of the poorest fifth of the population did not vote, compared to only 20 per cent of the richest fifth.

Just as importantly though, if voters are no longer choosing a major party on the basis of ideology, then the rationale for choosing one party over another changes. A number of recent books have suggested that 'valence politics' is now dominant. That means that voters don't vote on the basis of their self-interest and resulting ideological beliefs, but rather for parties that they believe to be competent managers – whether of the economy or public services. It is difficult to disagree that competency has become more important. The explanation is less clear cut however. Some say that this is due to the voters changing: the classless society that John Major envisaged, but did not achieve. Again, however, an alternative view is that it is the parties that have changed: the removal of class conflict from politics that Tony Blair envisaged and actually achieved by altering the policies that Labour offered the electorate. That has interesting implications for the future, as parties could choose to differentiate themselves from one another again leading to a renewed class basis to British politics. Or new parties could seek to appeal to the working-class voters who no longer feel represented by the mainstream parties, as some argue UKIP is now doing (see Chapter 44). Class is not dead in British politics; it may only be sleeping.

FURTHER READING

The findings discussed here are largely based on two articles: Geoff Evans and James Tilley's 'The depoliticization of inequality and redistribution: Explaining the decline of class voting' (*Journal of Politics*, 2012) and Geoff Evans and James Tilley's 'How parties shape class politics: Structural transformation, ideological convergence and the decline of class voting in Britain' (*British Journal of Political Science*, 2012) and an as yet unfinished book provisionally entitled *The New Class War* by James Tilley and Geoff Evans. For more information on 'valence politics' see *Performance Politics and the British Voter* by Harold Clarke et al. (Cambridge University Press, 2009) and for the original, and in many ways best, discussion of class and British politics see David Butler and Donald Stokes *Political Change in Britain* (Macmillan, 1974).

— CHAPTER 35 —

The average voter is a woman: sex and gender differences

Rosie Campbell

A staple of every election is a discussion of the 'women's vote', as if women are distinct from the 'normal' votes cast. Given that women make up 51 per cent of the population – and are just as likely to vote as men – the average voter is in fact a woman.

Historically, average voters have tended to be slightly more Conservative than male voters, although New Labour managed to reduce this advantage by picking up the votes of younger women, particularly middle and higher income mothers. There are larger sex differences in support for some of the smaller parties: about two-thirds of BNP voters are men and the SNP and UKIP also receive more support from men than women. Women are also disproportionately represented among undecided voters and they tend to make up their minds who to vote for closer to election day. For example in April 2010, just one month before the general election, 16 per cent of women compared to 6 per cent of men said they didn't know who they would vote for. Women say that they are less interested in politics than men (48 per cent of men and 32 per cent of women reported being interested in politics in 2010), although this gap is reversed when they are asked how interested they are in specific policy areas such as education or health. Women are also more likely to select the 'Don't know' option in political attitude questions and on average score slightly lower than men on political knowledge measures. But in the end, women are just as likely to vote as men. Indeed, in raw terms, women are slightly more likely to vote than men, although this is due to women's greater longevity combined with higher levels of electoral participation among the old; turnout among women and men of the same age is pretty similar. The growing 'grey' vote is much more a female vote than the electorate overall.

There are also consistent sex differences in some political attitudes. Women tend to favour increased taxation and spending on public services more often than men and they are less likely to support cuts in expenditure on key public services (health and education in particular), perhaps unsurprisingly as such spending cuts have a larger impact on women than men. Women have more egalitarian views than men on a number of issues; they tend to be more progressive on gender equality and less often colour prejudiced or homophobic than men. And there are differences in what political scientists call salience, the priority men and women attach to particular topics. Women report more concern about education and health than men and men give relations with the EU and taxation greater priority.

All of the above is well-documented. But the truth about women voters is more inconvenient for those of us who would find it easier to trot out a simple story about what women want. The reality is that there is no single story to tell about women voters. They are not some homogenous group that party strategists can target with ease; they are as divided in their opinions as men are. Moreover, although there are differences between women and men in their political behaviour, the similarities are much stronger and more interesting. The truth is that female voters are largely the same as male voters.

Take vote choice, for example. Although there are differences, since the late '70s, the overall gap in vote choice has become very small. The figure illustrates the gender gap in support for the two main parties from 1945–2010; it is calculated as the difference between the Con-Lab lead for women and for men. A positive score indicates that men are more likely to vote Conservative, a negative score that women are more likely to do so. The decline in Conservative leanings among women voters is obvious, and since 1974 this gap has rarely reached statistical significance. Given the numbers involved, these differences may still affect the election outcome, but it also means that they are small enough that variations in the direction of the gender gap in individual surveys can be produced by random error.

THE BRITISH GENDER GAP 1964–2010

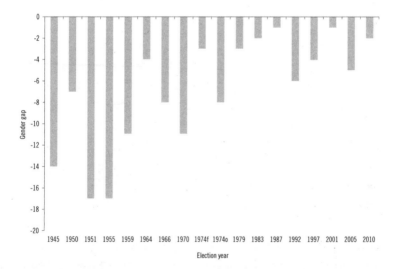

Similarly, although there are differences in their political priorities, men and women's political priorities both move with the national issue attention cycle. In 2001 and 2005, for example, women consistently rated health or education as the most important issue facing Britain more often than men did, whereas more men than women were most concerned about the economy. But as men become more concerned with the economy following the 2007 financial crisis, so did women. By 2010 both men and women ranked the economy as more important than either health or education, by a long way. Women may still be slightly more concerned than men about health or education, and men slightly more concerned than women about the economy, but the differences are tiny. There are underlying differences in political preferences but both men's and women's priorities move with the national mood and quite substantial sex gaps can be reduced to negligible levels by major events that shift the nation's priorities.

Women's hostility to public spending cuts relative to men's suggests that women may have a marginally different view as to how the economic crisis should be managed. But even here the average sex gap in support for spending cuts is around 8 percentage points, a sizeable gap but certainly not a chasm. Targeting women as a homogenous block is unlikely to be a successful election strategy for political parties; perhaps re-conceiving the average voter so that she is a woman might be.

FURTHER READING

For a full discussion of the history of the gender gap in Britain see Pippa Norris's 'Gender: a gender-generation gap?' in *Critical Elections: British Parties and Voters in Long-Term Perspective* (Sage, 1999). Other useful sources on gender and voting in Britain are Rosie Campbell's *Gender and the Vote in Britain* (ECPR Press, 2006) and her 'What do we really know about women voters? Gender, elections and public opinion' (*Political Quarterly*, 2012). For an analysis of the relationship between gender and the vote in an international context, see Ronald Inglehart and Pippa Norris's 'The developmental theory of the gender gap: women and men's voting behaviour in global perspective' (*International Political Science Review*, 2000).

CHAPTER 36

Why ethnic minorities vote Labour: group norms

Anthony Heath

Peter Pulzer once famously wrote 'Class is the basis of British politics; all else is embellishment and detail.' Those days are long since gone, and one of the embellishments has now overtaken class as the most powerful social cleavage in British politics: ethnic background is now a much more powerful predictor of how people will vote than is social class (or region, or age, or indeed any other social division). At the 2010 general election Labour won only 29 per cent of the popular vote while the Conservatives won 36 per cent – an overall Conservative lead of seven points. Labour did slightly better in the working class, where 41 per cent voted Labour and 31 per cent voted Conservative – a Labour lead of ten points. In striking contrast 68 per cent of ethnic minority voters gave their support to Labour, and only 16 per cent supported the Conservatives – a whopping lead of fifty-two points.

The remarkable Labour loyalty of ethnic minorities could have major long-term implications for the party system as Britain's minority communities are growing rapidly, and are set to become a larger and larger proportion of the electorate in the future.

How are we to explain this overwhelming support for Labour? One of the standard accounts of vote choice focuses on matching voters' policy preferences to parties' policy offers. On this account, voters will back the party which has policies most in tune with their preferences on the issues they care about most. This is the basis for the argument for example that, in order to woo voters back from UKIP, the Conservative Party should toughen up its stance on immigration, so that it is more in line with what voters want.

So we could try to explain minority support for the Labour Party by the extent of fit between the party's and minorities' positions on the issues to which minorities give highest priority. If minorities have distinctive policy preferences, and if Labour policy is closely in tune with these preferences, then this could potentially explain their support for the party. The table below shows how minorities and the white British compare on a number of major issues.

PERCENTAGE FAVOURING THE 'PROGRESSIVE' SIDE OF THE DEBATE

	WHITE BRITISH	ETHNIC MINORITIES
Spending on health and services	49	37
Redistributing wealth	66	45
Allowing strong trade unions	62	56
Protecting rights of the accused	15	22
Detention without trial	33	57
Sending asylum seekers home	39	50
War in Afghanistan	64	56

The table shows some differences – although not in the expected direction: on the classic 'left–right' issues which have historically divided the electorate such as government spending and the redistribution of wealth, minorities are actually less 'leftist' than the white British.

To be sure, minorities are considerably more progressive on detention without trial and on asylum seekers, although these were not issues on which the actual Labour governments of Tony Blair and Gordon Brown were especially progressive. If anything, these issues might lead minorities to oppose Labour policy. The only issue on which minorities were more likely than the white British to support Labour policy was on the war in Afghanistan, although on this issue there were major differences between different minority groups. So on this evidence, it is not obvious that minorities would actually support Labour at all on the basis of the party's policies, and certainly not by the huge margins described earlier.

Perhaps we are thinking about the issue in the wrong way, however. Voters might not focus on a party's policies right now, but instead consider the whole history of their experiences with different parties. Mo Fiorina once wrote that: 'Citizens are not fools. Having often observed political equivocation, if not outright lying, should they listen carefully to campaign promises? ... In order to ascertain whether the incumbents have performed poorly or well, citizens need only calculate the changes in their own welfare.'

Fiorina's argument was that voters judge what parties have actually done for them in the past, updating their 'tallies' as they go along, giving more weight to recent experiences but still attaching some importance to events long ago. This offers a more promising account of minority support for Labour. All the landmark legislation designed to protect minority interests, such as the 1965, 1968 and 1976 Race Relations Acts, and the 2000 Race Relations (Amendment) Act, have been passed under Labour governments, while Conservative governments have been notable for their legislation restricting entry rights and making access to citizenship more difficult (with a complete failure to tackle discrimination), legislation which has not gone down well with minority voters whose families may often be adversely affected.

These histories of the parties' engagement, or lack of engagement, with minority concerns must be a major part of the story. However, it is not at all clear whether Fiorina's emphasis on the individual citizen's own experiences is right. On an individualistic account, we would expect that a migrant who had only recently arrived in Britain, and who therefore had had little personal experience of Labour's past efforts to improve minority welfare, would be much less likely to support the party than a longer-established voter who had seen and experienced the changes brought about, for example, by the landmark 1976 act.

In line with the theory, we find that migrants who arrived in Britain a long time ago are slightly more likely to support Labour than the most recent arrivals, whose main experience was of New Labour. But even the most recent arrivals coming to Britain in the first decade of the twenty-first century, were still overwhelmingly Labour supporters.

So we have to find an explanation which can account for the Labour loyalties of newly arrived ethnic minority voters. Individualistic explanations clearly fail, and hence the natural alternative is to turn to explanations which take account of the social milieu in which voters find themselves. When a migrant arrives in Britain, he or she will typically be joining an established ethnic community, which will have developed over time many shared norms and sentiments. Migrants do not have to wait to find out for themselves what life would be like under different governments; they will quickly pick up ideas about the British political situation from their new community. Community norms and sentiments, then, may well perpetuate the belief, based on collective experience, that Labour looks after ethnic minorities while the Conservatives do not. And new arrivals will be introduced to these ideas, rather than having to acquire the information for themselves.

Group-based explanations of this kind have become much less popular than they once were, reflecting not only changes in intellectual fashion towards more individualistic choice-based theories but also reflecting real changes in British society, which has seen the disappearance of distinctive class-based communities based around heavy industries, and the rise of more fragmented and mobile careers. But while communities based on social class may have declined or weakened, there are undoubtedly strong communities based on ethnicity in Britain today.

FURTHER READING

A full treatment of this topic, and an account of the data on which it is based, can be found in Chapter 6 of *The Political Integration of Ethnic Minorities in Britain* by Anthony Heath et al. (Oxford University Press, 2013). Previous important studies include Shamit Saggar's *Race and Representation: Electoral politics and ethnic pluralism in Britain* (Manchester University Press, 2000) and Tariq Modood's *Multicultural Politics: Racism, ethnicity and Muslims in Britain* (Edinburgh University Press, 2005).

CHAPTER 37

Learning to be British by being a grumpy voter: ethnic minority turnout

Gemma Rosenblatt

Many black and ethnic minority immigrants to Britain have a strong belief in the duty to vote and high levels of trust in the British political system. In contrast, British-born second and third generation black and ethnic minority voters are more sceptical in their assessment of the political system – with views more closely in line with those of the white British electorate. And yet, as the political scepticism of the second-plus generations increases, so does their likelihood to vote in elections, contrary to everything we know about why people do or don't vote. There is a move from cheery abstention among migrants to grumpy voting among their children and grandchildren. It's very British.

A key finding in research on voter turnout is that seeing voting as a civic duty strongly predicts higher turnout in elections. Some 85 per cent of Britons who believed in the duty to vote cast a ballot at the 2005 general election, compared to only 50 per cent of those who believed 'people should only vote if they care who wins'. Polling from the 2010 general election found that 91 per cent of first generation migrants of Indian, Pakistani, Bangladeshi, black Caribbean and black African origin agreed that it was every citizen's duty to vote – compared to 78 per cent of those classed as white British. On this basis, you would expect turnout among black and ethnic minority citizens who came to this country as first generation migrants to be at least as high as turnout among the white British population.

Yet validated turnout at the 2010 election was noticeably lower among the first generation groups (53 per cent) than it was among those classed as white British (70 per cent). Even factoring in that 5 per cent of the migrant group were not eligible to be on the register, there is still a significant difference in turnout and an even bigger difference in the correlation between belief in the duty to vote and turnout. This makes a belief in the duty to vote a much weaker predictor of turnout among first generation migrants than it is for the white British population.

Let's consider another determinant of turnout. Satisfaction with democracy and trust in the political system are also associated with higher turnout in elections. Yet looking at the views of first and second-plus generations of migrants indicates that here, also, the relationship isn't the same as it is for native-born white voters. Among the five black and ethnic minority communities mentioned above, 77 per cent of those who moved to Britain as adults reported that they were satisfied with democracy, notably higher than the 59 per cent recorded for the white British population. Trust in politics is also an area that receives higher ratings among the first generation migrants: the levels of trust in Parliament at the time of the 2010 general election was 50 per cent for first generation migrants, compared to 34 per cent for white British. Similarly, trust in politicians was at 43 per cent, compared to 24 per cent for white British. So first generation migrants trust politicians, are satisfied with democracy, and believe turning out to vote is an important civic duty. Yet they are much less likely to vote in elections.

These figures challenge our established thinking around the strength of the relationship between satisfaction with democracy and turnout. Clearly, the voting decision works differently for migrant voters than for other citizens. But this difference is not sustained among the native-born children and grandchildren of migrants: such voters come to resemble the white British majority in their behaviour, and in what predicts it. Fewer among them believe in the duty to vote (81 per cent). They are less likely to be satisfied with democracy (52 per cent). They are less trusting of Parliament (26 per cent), and also of politicians (20 per cent). For someone who believes in democracy, this all sounds pretty worrying. And yet, they're also more likely to vote than the first generation of migrants, which is a bit of a conundrum. What is it that sets migrant voters apart?

First generation migrants come from a variety of different countries that may be more or less democratised. It's possible that it takes time to participate in, or adapt to, the electoral practices of the UK. Sometimes the practical steps, such as registering to vote, may not be a priority or an area of familiarity. Moreover, maybe the views of first generation migrants and their actual behaviour are not as out of sync as this data indicates. It's not difficult to imagine that those who have moved to Britain from abroad may feel more social pressure to give the responses they think people want to hear, in order to 'fit in' in their new home. The generations that follow them may be less concerned about this. They may also be more conscious of living in a society where turnout is on the decline and it is socially acceptable to admit to not believing in a civic duty to vote.

We cannot be sure, therefore, whether the extent to which the relationship between the perception of a duty to vote and actually turning out to vote on election day is weakened by the first generation black and ethnic minority communities living in Britain or whether they are just too polite to tell researchers what they really think. We can be more sure, however, that the views and actions of second-plus generations begin to merge with those of the white British community and, as a result, these voters' voices are heard more clearly in the political system than that of their migrant ancestors. Is it better to be a grumpy voter than a happy non-voter?

FURTHER READING

Much of the data in this chapter came from the Ethnic Minority British Election Study. It collected information following the 2010 general election on the social and political attitudes, electoral behaviour, and political integration of major established ethnic minorities in Britain – namely people of Indian, Pakistani, Bangladeshi, black Caribbean, and black African background. Many of the findings from the study are examined by Anthony Heath et al. in *The Political Integration of Ethnic Minorities in Britain* (Oxford University Press, 2013). The British Social Attitudes survey is also a helpful guide to monitoring trends in the belief of a civic duty to vote over the last thirty years. Much of the data is now available free online.

—CHAPTER 38—

Disengaged youth:
age and political engagement

Alison Park

The run-up to every general election is now accompanied by a lot of hand-wringing about falling levels of political engagement and the particularly low levels found among young people. But haven't young people always been less engaged with politics, developing a taste for it as they get older and start grappling with 'adult' life in the form of jobs, taxes, parenthood, housing and so on?

It's certainly true that younger people are less engaged with politics than older groups. A recent Hansard Society report found only a quarter (24 per cent) of those aged eighteen to twenty-four were certain they would vote in an immediate general election, half the rate found among the population as a whole (49 per cent). There are clear age differences in the extent to which people support or feel close to a particular political party (known as their party identification); the 2013 British Social Attitudes survey found 61 per cent of those aged eighteen to twenty-four identified with a party, compared with 83 per cent of those aged sixty-five and over. Young people are also less interested in politics and less likely to have undertaken any political activities.

But what do age differences like these actually mean? To tease out their significance we have to grapple with a distinction between what the academic literature describes as 'generational', 'life-cycle' and 'period' differences.

Generational differences exist between particular generations *and persist as each generation gets older*. These sorts of differences will lead to clear shifts in social attitudes over time, as older generations die out and are replaced by younger ones with very different views.

By contrast, life-cycle differences relate to people's chronological age. They exist where we find people's views or experiences *changing as they get older and/or encounter particular life events*. If people do become more interested in politics and more likely to form an allegiance to a particular political party this would be an example of a life-cycle influence.

Finally there are period influences. These are major events that *affect everyone in a society at a particular time* and which are likely to have a considerable impact on many people's views, irrespective of their age or generation.

These differences may sound fairly trivial, but they matter hugely when it comes to thinking about what age differences in political engagement imply for the future. If political engagement is an example of a generational difference, these findings point towards a Britain that will become steadily less engaged with politics. But if they are an example of life-cycle differences then they do not necessarily herald any future change at all, as the currently disaffected young will gradually engage as they get older. And if the age differences we see now are period effects, then while the voters who have grown up in the current cynical climate may well retain that cynicism, subsequent generations growing up in different conditions may take different views.

To explore this, each line in the graph shows the proportion of people in a particular generation (defined as those born in a particular decade) who identify with a particular political party and how this has changed over the last thirty years. To make it clearer, it just presents data for those generations born since the '30s.

PERCENTAGE OF PEOPLE IDENTIFYING WITH A POLITICAL PARTY, 1983–2013

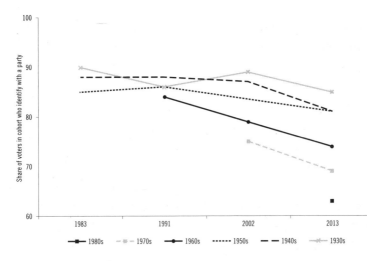

Source: British Social Attitude 1983–2013

The graph shows that each cohort is less likely to identify with any of the available political parties now than they were when they were younger. Take, for example, the '60s generation; in 1991 (when they were in their twenties), 84 per cent identified with a political party but now 74 per cent do so. This is important because it runs counter to evidence published in the '60s that party identification increases with age, and contradicts the common intuition that voters become more engaged in politics as they age. In Britain, over the past few decades, the opposite has happened. The graph also shows that each generation is less likely to identify with a political party than its predecessors. This is at its starkest in relation to those born in the '80s, among whom just 63 per cent identified with a party in 2013 (when they were aged twenty-four to thirty-three). This is far lower than was the case among the '60s generation; when they were at a similar age (in 1991), 84 per cent identified with a party.

So the extent to which people have an allegiance with a particular political party has declined among all generations (which is an example of a period effect) and is also notably lower among those born in more recent decades (a generational difference). As a result, the very small gap in party identification that existed between different generations in 1983 has steadily grown, and now stands at a very considerable 22 percentage points. Taken together, these changes help account for the fact that fewer people in Britain now identify with a political party: overall levels of identification have gone from 87 per cent in 1983 to 73 per cent in 2013.

Throughout the period for which we have data, young people have always been less engaged in politics than older ones. In that sense then, Britain's youth have always been politically disengaged. However, while some forms of political engagement (like interest in politics) might increase as people get older, this is not the case with party identification. As this gulf is a product of deep-seated generational trends, it is likely to carry on growing unless something major disrupts it, and will gradually drag down overall levels of engagement with political parties. Russell Brand's apathetic generation is currently the exception in British politics, but in time, perhaps they will become the norm.

FURTHER READING

There is further discussion of generational differences in political engagement in Lucy Lee and Penny Young's 'A disengaged Britain? Political interest and participation over

30 years', in *British Social Attitudes 30* (NatCen, 2013). There is a more detailed (and far more statistical!) discussion of party identification in Britain in David Sanders's 'The dynamics of party identification' in *Political Choice in Britain* (OUP, 2004). The Hansard Society's annual *Audit of Political Engagement* is an excellent source of material on engagement more generally.

CHAPTER 39

The policy few people want remains irresistible: lowering the voting age

Andrew Russell

I n 2004 the Electoral Commission's Age of Electoral Majority review recommended the minimum voting age should remain eighteen. Three years later the government reopened the debate and set up the Youth Citizenship Commission (YCC), which also found against reducing the voting age to sixteen.

The voting age is one of the few elements of the constitution that most voters know and support. The Hansard Society's *Audit of Political Engagement* shows better knowledge of the voting age than any other aspect of political awareness. Electoral Commission surveys have found the public firmly against lowering the voting age, with even a small majority of the principal beneficiaries – those aged fifteen to eighteen – against it. The YCC reported similar levels of hostility from the public and only lukewarm support among those aged sixteen to seventeen. A 2013 YouGov survey revealed that 60 per cent of the public are still against lowering the voting age.

Yet the movement towards reform seems irresistible. The Lib Dems,

SNP, Plaid Cymru, Greens and now Labour have all moved to support votes at sixteen. There have been several attempts to bring laws to reduce the voting age in Westminster and the enfranchisement of sixteen- and seventeen-year-olds in the Scottish Independence Referendum makes further reform likely.

Internationally Argentina, Austria, Brazil, Cuba, Ecuador and Nicaragua allow voting for all at sixteen. However the experience of these countries offers scant encouragement. Even in Austria (the place where proponents of the change are most likely to urge us to look) there is little evidence that sixteen- to seventeen-year-olds are more engaged than eighteen-year-olds. A notable study of vote intention for the 2009 Euro Parliament elections found Austrians under eighteen were the least certain of all age groups to vote.

Local experiments in some German regions (often connected to futile attempts to keep the SPD in power) and Norway haven't produced more engaged young citizens. In Argentina, Brazil and Ecuador, voting is compulsory for over-eighteens but not for those aged between sixteen and seventeen. Nearer home the reduction of the voting age in the Isle of Man was disastrous. Under one-fifth of eligible sixteen- to seventeen-year-olds actually voted in the 2006 Tynwald elections. Just in case you thought that was an unlucky episode, less than one-third voted in 2011 (against a Manx average of 57 per cent both times).

So there must be another source of support. But if you think there is a raft of rights gained at sixteen making an overwhelming case for enfranchisement, think again.

Lord Adonis recently repeated many of the most familiar claims: 'Given that sixteen-year-olds are judged old enough to leave home, to marry, to lead an independent life, and even join the Army, it is hard to argue in the modern age that they shouldn't also have the vote'. However a rudimentary fact check shows that each of Lord Adonis's claims is fallacious.

Very few sixteen- and seventeen-year-olds leave home nowadays (ONS figures show more than 90 per cent of them lived with parents in 2012) and those that do must rely on someone aged eighteen or over to sign a tenancy agreement for them.

According to the latest official figures, 92 per cent of sixteen- to seventeen-year-olds now stay in education. Furthermore the English law raising the Participation Age means that from 2015 young people *must* stay in education or training tied to formal educational qualifications until aged eighteen, which will further reduce the proportion of economically active and tax-paying sixteen- to seventeen-year-olds.

The 'no taxation without representation' mantra is often used in support of votes at sixteen but high tax thresholds and poor youth wages mean under one-tenth of under-eighteens actually earn enough to pay income tax. Anyway, why single out direct taxation? The Boston Tea Party protested about *indirect tax*; and indirect taxation applies to all consumers whether eight, twelve, sixteen or seventy-eight.

Those under eighteen need parental permission to marry in England, Wales and Northern Ireland. Moreover the number of young marriages has fallen dramatically over fifty years. In England and Wales in 1959 there were 184 weddings of boys, and 3,973 marriages involving girls, aged sixteen. In 2009 there were just eighteen weddings of boys, and eighty-eight of girls aged sixteen.

The Protocol of the UN Convention of the Human Rights of the Child means armed forces volunteers are kept out of active service until eighteen. Recruitment at sixteen (but only with parental permission) continues but this seems a very good argument for raising the age for enlisting rather than lowering the voting age.

Enfranchising sixteen- and seventeen-year-olds might also threaten key social protections they currently enjoy: local authority responsibility to shelter under-eighteens presenting as homeless might be undermined if they are considered full citizens. In recent years UK legislation has raised to eighteen the age at which tobacco and fireworks can be bought, tattoos done, or tanning booths visited. The age of consensual sex has reduced to sixteen but even then one party cannot be in a 'position of trust' over the other if they are under nineteen. These various age thresholds have made eighteen the de facto recognised age of UK adulthood.

Perhaps the political class sees the possibility of electoral advantage? Harold Wilson's government felt that reducing the voting age from twenty-one to eighteen in 1969 would benefit them – unless young Scots turned to the SNP. Maybe it's difficult to deny the claims of an organised and connected set of people who are continually said to be the future of the parties themselves. The Votes@16 coalition is certainly engaged but as the YCC concluded they might not accurately represent the constituency they speak for – the distance between the views of engaged and disengaged youth is enormous and growing.

The process of lowering the voting age is hard to stop once it has begun. Public opinion, international experiments and a move to enshrine eighteen as the age of adulthood ought to have consigned the idea of lowering the voting age to the political junkyard but yet it is still gathering momentum. It may happen because it's cheap, looks radical and encouraged by some organisations poised to benefit from the change.

FURTHER READING

For a brief overview of the academic literature around this subject start with one anti-reform study by Tak Wing Chan and Matthew Clayton – 'Should the voting age be lowered to sixteen?' (*Political Studies*, 2006) – and one pro-reform piece by Markus Wagner et al. – 'Voting at 16: Turnout and the quality of vote choice' (*Electoral Studies*, 2012). The Electoral Commission's *Age of Electoral Majority Report* (2004) and the *YCC Report* (2007) are both excellent at setting the context of the debate. Richard Crossman's *Diaries of a Cabinet Minister (1975–77)* provide the backdrop to the last lowering of the voting age in the UK.

—CHAPTER 40—

Another victim of the dodgy dossier: the Iraq War and the democratic faith of young people

Stuart Fox

The tenth anniversary of the invasion of Iraq was marked in the media by a revival of many of the debates which had raged a decade earlier. Was the war legal? Was it all about oil? Is Tony Blair a war criminal? These were joined by a new claim, however, with a number of those opposed to the war suggesting it had done permanent harm to Britain's political health, by turning a generation of young voters against the political system which ignored them and had gone to war.

Journalists like Owen Jones suggested that the decision by Tony Blair's government to support the US-led invasion, despite some of the largest street protests in generations, had fatally undermined the political faith of Britain's newest voters. Jones argued in *The Independent* that 'Iraq ... exploded what trust millions had in our political establishment', and that this was why young people are now so much less likely to vote than their elders. Laurie Penny, writing in the *New Statesman*, lamented the 'life-changing' sense of 'betrayal' now felt by all young people who marched against the war, and who now had no faith that organised political participation mattered or could influence decision-makers. Jones and Penny were joined by a chorus of others during the anniversary period, each sharing the view that the Iraq War was in some way responsible for the low political engagement of young people today. Sam Parker, for example, suggested that 'Tony Blair's hubris robbed a generation of their faith in politics' in the *Huffington Post*, while Andrew Murray described in *The Guardian* how British democracy had suffered a body blow from which it may never recover.

Measuring democratic faith is a lot harder than counting body bags – but we can look at three characteristics from several waves of the British Election Study which are central to our understanding of someone's faith in democracy: i) their interest in politics; ii) their view of how much influence they have on politics (otherwise called their 'political efficacy'); and iii) their satisfaction with the performance of the democratic system. If Britain's young people had suffered a crisis of democratic faith following the Iraq War (which took place between the 2001 and 2005 elections), we would expect to see their political interest, their political efficacy, and their satisfaction with British democracy fall sharply after 2001. Had the invasion killed off the faith of millions, as Jones and Penny suggest, then we would expect them to lose interest in politics, to no longer feel that they can influence it, and to become dissatisfied with the performance of the democratic system which had apparently betrayed them.

The figure puts this to the test, showing the percentage of those aged eighteen to twenty-four in Britain who had any interest at all in politics, who felt that they had at least some or a great deal of influence over decision-making, and who felt satisfied with the British democratic system, for the 2001, 2005 and 2010 general elections.

INDICATORS OF DEMOCRATIC FAITH AMONG THOSE AGED BETWEEN EIGHTEEN AND TWENTY-FOUR IN BRITAIN: 2001–10

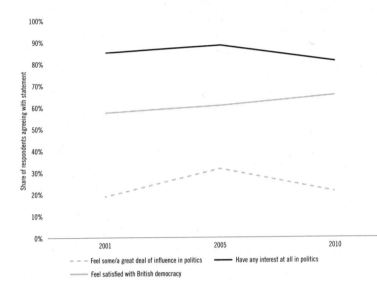

Source: British Election Study face-to-face survey, 2001, 2005 and 2010

There is little in here to support the theory that the Iraq War destroyed young people's faith in democracy. There is no evidence of a sharp decline in political interest or efficacy for new young cohorts entering the electorate between 2001 and 2010. In fact, those aged eighteen to twenty-four entering the electorate after the Iraq War were more satisfied with British democracy than their predecessors: in 2001 58 per cent were satisfied; by 2005 it was 60 per cent; and by 2010 it reached 66 per cent. Despite not only the war in Iraq, but also the expenses scandal and an almost unprecedented distrust of politicians, young people entering the electorate in 2005 and 2010 were more satisfied with British democracy than those in 2001.

What about those people who were aged eighteen to twenty-four in 2001, and saw the government take Britain to war in Iraq just two years after their first experience of voting in a general election? Did the war leave a scar on the democratic faith of this 'Iraq Generation'? Looking specifically at this group (that is, the cohort who were aged eighteen to twenty-four in 2001, and twenty-seven to thirty-two by 2010), we find that 81 per cent were interested in politics, 63 per cent felt they had an influence on politics, and 58 per cent were satisfied with British democracy in 2001. By 2010, 95 per cent were interested in politics, 58 per cent felt politically efficacious, and 60 per cent were satisfied with democracy. In other words, while the Iraq Generation became slightly less confident in their ability to influence politics after the war, they also became more interested in politics, and slightly more satisfied with British democracy than they were in 2001. Such changes are in line with our expectations based on what we know about how political attitudes change as voters age, but more importantly they provide no indication at all of a generation scarred for life after the Iraq War.

The idea that the invasion of Iraq, in the face of such massive and visible organised opposition – combined with the eventual failure to find any weapons of mass destruction – would damage the democratic faith of Britain's young people is quite easy to accept at face value. It is hard to believe that such a controversial event would have no impact on the democratic faith of British citizens, and no doubt it did do lasting damage to the faith of some. Nevertheless, a look at the data has shown that Owen Jones's and Laurie Penny's experiences were not representative of their generation; there is no evidence that the 2003 invasion of Iraq had any lasting negative consequences for the democratic faith of those who entered the electorate just a couple of years earlier (the Iraq generation), or of young people in Britain more generally.

FURTHER READING

Owen Jones's article 'What a tragedy that we couldn't stop the war in Iraq despite marching in our thousands' was in *The Independent* on 10 February 2013. Laurie Penny's article 'Ten years ago we marched against the Iraq War and I learned a lesson in betrayal' was in the *New Statesman* on 14 February 2014. More on the political attitudes of young people can be found in Matt Henn and Nick Foard's 'Young people, political participation and trust in Britain' (*Parliamentary Affairs*, 2012). David Sanders and colleagues wrote about the effect of the Iraq War on voters in 'Taking the bloom off New Labour's rose: party choice and voter turnout in Britain, 2005' (*Journal of Elections, Public Opinion and Parties*, 2006).

'No part of the education of a politician is more indispensable than the fighting of elections.'

WINSTON CHURCHILL, *GREAT CONTEMPORARIES*, 1937

—CHAPTER 41—

Withering grassroots: the problems of constituency campaigning

Ron Johnston

In 2013 the three main British political parties announced their battleground constituencies for the 2015 election: Labour identified 106 targets it needed to gain to deliver a majority; the Conservatives selected forty marginal seats they need to retain and a further forty potential gains to ensure a clear majority next time; and, alongside defending seats already held, the Liberal Democrats identified fifty further seats for intensive campaigning. Campaigning there started almost immediately, and intensified over the subsequent months; elsewhere the parties and their candidates will be much less in evidence.

The parties' local branches perform the grunt-work of the ground war in the constituencies: maintaining databases of likely supporters with whom contact should pay dividends; raising money to pay for leaflets, posters and other items; and recruiting volunteers (party activists and supporters) to deliver leaflets and knock on doors. But strategy is decided nationally and regionally.

Almost all of the money spent locally is raised locally, however, through fundraising events, donations and – for some fortunate branches – other sources such as rents from buildings they own. Some local parties (though rarely for Labour) receive central party contributions – mainly for laying the foundations rather than the final burst of spending.

Most locally raised money is spent, directly or indirectly, on contacting likely supporters. During the last month of the 2010 campaign, Conservative, Labour and Liberal Democrat candidates together spent some £7.4 million on leaflets and similar unsolicited materials. Where Labour candidates spent more than 75 per cent of the allowed maximum in a seat, for example, 55 per cent of electors surveyed by the British Election Study (BES) received at least one of their leaflets; where they spent less than 25 per cent, only half as many received any leaflets – a difference that also characterised the other two parties.

Around 40 per cent of BES respondents were contacted by at least one party in 2010, some 30 per cent by two of them, and 25 per cent by all three. Leaflets were by far the most common form of contact: less than 10 per cent reported being visited at home by a canvasser, and less than 5 per cent were contacted by phone or email. Those contacted were concentrated in marginal seats and had already been identified as potential supporters. They were more likely to vote for the party than were others not contacted. For example, 80 per cent of those who voted Labour in 2005 and who intended to support the party again in 2010 before the official campaign started, but then received no subsequent contact, actually voted Labour; of those contacted by leaflet plus some other means the percentage voting Labour increased to 90 per cent; and with more contacts still the figure increased to 96 per cent.

But local parties find raising the funds to sustain such contacts increasingly difficult. All local parties whose annual turnover exceeds £25,000 must return audited accounts to the Electoral Commission. In

2010, 359 Conservative constituency parties exceeded that threshold, compared to just eighty each for Labour and the Liberal Democrats.

THE AVERAGE PERCENTAGE OF THE MAXIMUM ALLOWED SPENT BY LABOUR AND CONSERVATIVE CANDIDATES AT GENERAL ELECTIONS 1959–2010, ACCORDING TO CONSTITUENCY MARGINALITY

ELECTION MARGIN	LABOUR					CONSERVATIVE				
	1959	1983	1997	2005	2010	1959	1983	1997	2005	2010
SEATS WON (%)										
20 +	77	71	70	68	63	92	84	88	80	71
11–20	86	77	80	82	78	97	88	90	79	74
6–10	95	87	84	91	79	98	89	94	83	84
0–5	99	90	90	87	75	99	90	88	88	89
SEATS LOST (%)										
0–5	99	82	93	74	60	99	83	86	91	89
6–10	97	83	92	48	45	93	76	80	88	89
11–20	88	72	90	35	28	83	68	58	81	82
20 +	66	45	58	26	16	69	42	38	42	39

This shows in their campaigning expenditure and in the number of contacts with potential voters. Candidate spending is legally limited during the final weeks of the official campaign – a maximum of around £12,000 depending on the constituency electorate. The table shows average expenditure by Labour and Conservative candidates, as a percentage of the local maximum, according to the seat's marginality after the preceding election. In 1959 Labour spending averaged just below the maximum in seats it either lost or won in 1955 by margins of less than 5 percentage points. By 2010, it averaged only 75 per cent in those won by a similar margin in 2005 and just 60 per cent where it lost. Conservative spending didn't fall away as much as Labour's in its marginal seats but neither spent as much in 'hopeless' seats where victory was extremely unlikely in 2010 as they had fifty years before. Less was being spent (in real terms even less than the numbers suggest, since the maxima were not increased in line with inflation); and it was increasingly focused on a smaller proportion of constituencies. Parties were less active at turning out the vote where they were sure they would lose and even where they hoped to win they found it increasingly difficult to raise all they were allowed to spend there. Increasingly, therefore, candidates have depended on what their central party organisations decide to send directly to potential supporters (recorded in increasingly sophisticated databases, mainly compiled through telephone polling) – plus as much volunteer labour as they can mobilise to sustain their efforts on the ground.

The increasing focus of campaign activity in the most marginal seats, while efficient for resource-strapped parties, is not such good news for engaging all voters in the electoral process. General election campaigns used to be characterised by large and lively public meetings: there are very few now. The streets were full of posters and canvassers handing-out and delivering leaflets: many constituencies are now virtually poster-free and their electors ignored by parties largely unconcerned with whether they bother to vote. General elections are won and lost in less than one-quarter of all constituencies, and attention focuses on the swing voters in those swing seats only. Parties and candidates engage with fewer and fewer voters elsewhere.

FURTHER READING

On the financial health of local parties and their campaign expenditure, see Ron Johnston and Charles Pattie's *Money and Electoral Politics: Local Parties and Funding at*

General Elections (Policy Press, 2014). For analyses of the extent, nature and impact of local campaigns see 'We've got them on the list: contacting, canvassing and voting in a British general election campaigning' by Ron Johnston et al. (*Electoral Studies,* 2012). On the benefits of early campaigning, see 'Laying the foundations for electoral success: Conservative pre-campaign canvassing before the 2010 general election' by David Cutts et al. (*Journal of Elections, Public Opinion and Parties,* 2012).

CHAPTER 42

Can't buy me votes (necessarily): money and elections

Justin Fisher

Party finance has been a fairly constant source of debate in recent years. Despite the introduction of the Political Parties, Elections and Referendums Act 2000 (PPERA) – an extensive piece of legislation which introduced hitherto unheard of levels of transparency, regulation and oversight into British party finance – this was anything but the end of the story. Since then, several extensive reports and further legislation have not brought about a settled situation and party political finance remains a problem that refuses to be solved. Two myths run through all these attempted reforms. The first is that parties spend too much money on elections and that this spending should be reduced. The second is that money buys votes, and that parties that spend more money will therefore win more votes.

We have had caps on election spending since 1883. Back then, there was no national campaign to speak of and so the caps applied to candidate spending in constituencies. National campaign spending has only been capped since PPERA. That limited national party spending for the 365 days before polling day at a rate of £30,000 per constituency contested. For the major parties contesting all of the seats in Britain in 2015 the spending limit will therefore be just shy of £19 million. But the figure of £30,000 per constituency has never been adjusted for inflation, so the amount the parties are allowed to spend in real terms is steadily falling: £19 million will buy around a third less in 2015 than it did in 2000; in real terms it equates to around £13 million at 2000 prices.

In addition, most central party expenditure is not on elections; campaign spending over a four-year period either side of an election only accounts for around 20 per cent of the total expenditure by the three main parties. Even in the year of the last general election, the main parties only spent on average around 35 per cent of their total expenditure on campaigning. The rest goes on routine party activity. Big money is therefore not a growing problem in British politics – in fact the sums parties are allowed to spend at elections are steadily declining.

The second myth is that money buys votes. Of course, leaflets, posters, broadcast production and the like all need to be paid for. But the argument that because X party spends more than Y party, then X will automatically perform better electorally is often wide of the mark. In terms of national expenditure, there is little evidence that a financial advantage at national level will always lead to an electoral one. One study over thirty-five years examining annual expenditure and poll ratings suggested that there was only one circumstance where increased party spending could improve popularity: Conservative spending when it was the incumbent party. The advantage was relatively small – the party would have had to spend the equivalent of nearly £2 million extra every year to gain an estimated electoral advantage of 0.4 per cent. And, if just we look at the 2010 election, the Conservatives had a significant financial advantage, spending £16.7 million compared with Labour's £8 million and the Liberal Democrats' £4.8 million. Yet, of course, the Conservatives' electoral advantage was nowhere near as large as its financial one.

At constituency level, the picture is a bit more complicated. There is consistent evidence over time that candidates that spend more tend to perform better electorally, particularly when they are challengers. In 2010, for example, had Conservative candidates spent the maximum possible in every seat and both Labour and Liberal Democrat spent very little, the Conservatives would have won an estimated 344 seats, enough for a small but working Commons majority. A similar scenario where Labour candidates spent the maximum and other parties mounted minimal campaigns would have produced an estimated 282 seats for Labour compared with 292 for the Conservatives. However, what candidate spending fails to capture is voluntary effort, the labour provided for free by party activists and supporters. When this is factored in, the positive electoral effects of higher spending can be offset by the free campaigning delivered by those activists. Thus in 2010, we find that despite the Conservatives candidates' financial advantage, both Labour and Liberal Democrat candidates were able to counter this through their voluntary efforts, supplied for free. Had Labour campaigns engaged in the highest levels of free campaigning (as undertaken in their most intense campaigns) in every seat (with Conservative and Liberal Democrat campaigns being minimal), Labour would have won an estimated 350 seats. In other words, the effects of free campaigns can be greater than those based on money.

Money matters in politics, and it's perfectly sensible to restrict spending to some extent, not least to allow parties to spend more time on politics rather than fundraising. And, because of the (tremendously far-sighted) decision at the birth of commercial television not to permit party advertising on broadcast media, the cost is kept down anyway. But calls to restrict parties even more are based on myths and should be resisted. Not only that, further reductions in caps could present problems for the health of elections. While the sums spent by 'third parties' (campaigning groups that do not stand for election) is regulated, the spending of other key electoral actors like the media is not (nor should it be). The issue is that if parties can spend less on campaigns, they could easily find themselves unable to respond if campaigning on several fronts: against rival parties, third parties and hostile media campaigns. Since parties are the only ones actually standing for election, there is a good argument that they should not be so hamstrung as to be unable to respond to campaigns by those that are unaccountable to the electorate.

FURTHER READING

Details about the impact of national party spending can be found in Justin Fisher's 'Party Expenditure and Electoral Prospects: A National Level Analysis of Britain' (*Electoral Studies*, 1999). For specific coverage of the last election, see Justin Fisher's 'Party Finance – Normal Service Resumed?' (*Parliamentary Affairs*, 2010). A detailed examination of candidate spending in 2010 is contained in 'The Long and the Short of it: Local Campaigning at the British 2010 General Election' by Ron Johnston et al. (*Political Studies*, 2013) while a comparison of the impact of free campaigning and that which incurs cost is in 'You get what you (don't) pay for: The impact of volunteer labour and candidate spending at the 2010 British General Election' by Justin Fisher et al. (*Parliamentary Affairs*, 2014). A detailed study of public opinion on party finance can be found in Jennifer van Heerde-Hudson and Justin Fisher's 'Parties heed (with caution): Public knowledge of and attitudes towards party finance in Britain' (*Party Politics*, 2013).

—CHAPTER 43—

Definitely mature, not necessarily mad: party members

Tim Bale

Quite why, nobody really knows, but the one thing that everyone picked up on from the first academic survey of Conservative Party members ever conducted was that their average age was sixty-two.

That survey was conducted back in the '90s, along with surveys on Labour and the Lib Dems (which, incidentally, suggested that their members were slightly younger: forty-eight for Labour, fifty-nine for the Lib Dems). The survey was conducted with the full cooperation of the Conservative Party, but perhaps because of the negative publicity that it generated, it ended up being both the first time and the last time the Tories allowed the academics in. But that hasn't stopped us. Aided by the vast internet panels of people put together by companies like YouGov, political scientists are now able to survey the rank-and-file without having to ask the party's permission first.

In the summer of 2013, after analysing completed questionnaires from around 850 rank-and-file Conservatives (enough to give us almost as much confidence in our findings as we would have in the findings of the opinion polls we read every day), we found that the average Tory Party member was aged fifty-nine. Mature, then, but not quite as geriatric as some commentators (including, for instance, *The Observer*'s Andrew Rawnsley, who suggested in July of that year that the average age was 'about seventy-four') had assumed.

In some ways this shouldn't be a cause for concern for the party. For one thing, it suggests that the Conservative Party's membership isn't that bad a reflection of its supporters in the electorate. Most polls suggest that the average person saying they would vote Conservative is in their mid-to-late fifties.

For another, just because so many Conservative members are in the autumn (or perhaps late summer) of their years doesn't necessarily mean they have attitudes which cut them off from the rest of the electorate. It is tempting to portray the rank-and-file of the party – indeed, the rank-and-file of any party – as ideological zealots. What political scientists know as 'May's law of curvilinear disparity' holds that parties' grassroots are almost bound to be more radical than either their parliamentary representatives or their voters. It's a neat theory, and one that goes with the grain of common wisdom. The evidence, however, does not support it.

One of the key findings of the original surveys of party members in the '90s was that party members, of all parties, were not as extreme as they were often portrayed. This seems to remain the case, at least as far as the Conservatives are concerned. Rank-and-file Tory members' views on the vexed issue of immigration, in the survey in 2013, are much like those held by the general public: superficially hard-line but actually rather more nuanced than many imagine. True, a quarter of members (26 per cent) would like to see an immediate cessation of immigration from inside or outside the EU. But that figure is dwarfed by the two-thirds (67 per cent) who are happy for the government to allow people to come and live in the UK as long as they have a job or some other means of financial support.

The same goes for their views on the economy and public services. By no means all Tory rank-and-file members can be considered the shock troops of devil-take-the-hindmost, free-market capitalism. Between a fifth and a quarter of them believe, for example, that big business benefits owners at the expense of workers, that ordinary people don't get a fair share of the nation's wealth, and that there is one law for the rich and one for the poor. Moreover – especially where their own interests or those of their children and grandchildren are directly affected – grassroots Conservatives clearly see a role for the state: while there is widespread support for spending cuts, less than half of rank-and-file members support the rise in university tuition fees, while more than half of them don't want to see cuts made to the NHS.

That said, the fact that the Tory grassroots are getting on a bit may still present a problem. Partly that's because rank-and-file members are actually older than the average suggests: the average age of fifty-nine disguises the fact that getting on for two-thirds of the Tory grassroots are aged sixty and above, while another 22 per cent are aged between forty and fifty-nine and only 6 per cent are between eighteen and twenty-four years old. But it's also because they are probably older than those who belong to their main rival. True, we don't have equivalent figures for the Labour Party or the Lib Dems, but we've no obvious reason to think that the age gap which those initial surveys revealed has shrunk, and electoral and opinion research consistently shows higher support for Labour among younger people.

That might not be such bad news if the Tories were oldies but goldies, using all that precious retirement time on their hands in the service of their party. But the 2013 members' survey suggests that nearly half of all Conservative Party members (44 per cent) spend no time whatsoever on party activity in an average month – and it's not just campaigning and meetings; that includes social events too. Another third (30 per cent) devote no more than five hours a month of their time to party activity, however broadly that's defined. Plus, only 18 per cent of members say they were more active than they were five years ago, whereas 39 per cent say they do less now that they did back then.

On the upside, this isn't that bad when compared to the survey of Tory members conducted in the early '90s. Back then, some three-quarters (as opposed to nearly half today) put in no time at all, meaning there were even fewer people at the grassroots who could genuinely be called activists. On the downside, the comparison that really counts, of course, is not with the '90s but with members of the other parties right here, right now.

Neither the age nor the attitudes of the average Tory rank-and-file member are likely, in and of themselves, to put off the party's target voters should that member turn up on their doorstep asking for their support. The problem for the Tories will be getting that average member to turn up on the doorstep in the first place – or to staff a phone-bank or post on Twitter or Facebook. Whether Labour, whose members are almost certainly younger, and the Lib Dems, whose 'pavement politics' traditions mean (or have meant in the past at least) that they are more active, can do any better remains to be seen.

FURTHER READING

The first academic surveys of the Labour Party, the Conservatives and the Lib Dems were conducted by teams led by Paul Whiteley and Patrick Seyd and can be read about in four books: *Labour's Grassroots* (Clarendon Press, 1992), *True Blues* (Oxford

University Press, 1994), *New Labour's Grassroots* (Palgrave, 2002) and *Third Force Politics* (Oxford University Press, 2006). Sarah Childs and Paul Webb were the first to conduct a survey of the Tories using an internet panel, the findings from which can be read in their book *Sex, Gender and the Conservative Party* (Palgrave, 2011). The 2013 survey was conducted, again with the help of YouGov, by Tim Bale and Paul Webb, and is reported in various newspaper and journal articles. For more on May's Law, see Pippa Norris's 'May's Law of Curvilinear Disparity Revisited: Leaders, Officers, Members and Voters in British Political Parties' (*Party Politics*, 1995).

CHAPTER 44

Not who you think:
UKIP voters

Matthew Goodwin

For the last thirty years radical right parties have been emerging all over Europe, pushing a nationalist, Eurosceptic and anti-immigration message. One of the greatest ironies of the rise of UKIP – from a small single-issue pressure group formed in the office of an LSE professor in 1993 to their success in the 2014 European elections, where they topped the poll – is that the success of a party founded to take Britain out of Europe has ended up making the British party system look much more European.

Conventional wisdom would have you believe that UKIP and Nigel Farage are drawing their strength from middle-class, gin-and-tonic-guzzling Conservatives who are obsessed with the European Union, and angry with David Cameron for failing to tackle the Eurocrats and pushing a more socially liberal stance on issues like equal marriage. Between rounds of golf out in the shires, they spend most of their time complaining about bureaucrats in Brussels wasting British taxpayers' money and yearning nostalgically for the days when Margaret Thatcher swung her handbag in EU summits. 'On issue after issue', wrote the commentator Tim Montgomerie, 'Nigel Farage, the UKIP leader, is directly wooing unhappy Conservatives,' while other senior journalists like Peter Oborne label UKIP 'the Conservative Party in exile'.

UKIP VOTERS COMPARED, 2004–13 (%)

	UKIP	CONS	LAB	LIB DEMS	FULL SAMPLE
SOCIAL CLASS					
Professional/managerial middle-class	30	44	36	43	39
Routine non-manual (clerical, sales)	27	28	29	29	28
Working class/not worked/other	42	28	35	27	33
EDUCATION: AGE LEFT SCHOOL					
16 or younger	55	36	40	31	38
17 or 18	21	24	20	19	21
19 or older	24	40	40	50	41
GENDER					
Male	57	49	49	47	50
Female	43	51	51	53	50
AGE					
Under 35	12	24	28	32	26
35–54	31	32	38	33	34
55 +	57	44	34	35	39
ETHNICITY					
White	99.6	98.9	96.3	98.4	98.0
Non-white	0.4	1.1	3.7	1.6	2.0

Source: British Election Study Continuous Monitoring Study 2004–13

As is often the case, the conventional wisdom is way off the mark.

Yes, the party's base is very socially distinctive: but it is blue-collar, poorly educated, old, white and male. Far from a rebellion of the golf club, UKIP is Britain's most working-class party. Indeed, to find a party support base that is as disproportionately working-class you need to go back to the Labour Party in the early '80s, and the days of Michael Foot. Since 2010, the voters who have flocked to Farage look more like Old Labour than True Blue Tories; they are older white men, working-class, struggling financially and poorly educated. As the table shows, 55 per cent of UKIP's voters left school aged sixteen or earlier, over 60 per cent are men, almost the same percentage are aged over fifty-four and over 98 per cent are white.

UKIP have succeeded by winning over Britain's 'left behind' voters: groups in society who have long struggled to adapt to the global economy, who hold a very different set of values from the new, middle-class and professional majority, and who were hit the hardest by the post-2008 financial crisis. It is these groups that have provided Nigel Farage with electoral strength. The groups who are much less likely to find his revolt appealing are the professional middle-class, university graduates, the young and Britain's rapidly growing ethnic minorities.

It is, though, easy to understand where the popular stereotype of UKIPers as angry middle-class Tories came from. UKIP began as a single-issue anti-EU pressure group, which emerged from the centre-right Eurosceptic fringe and in the early days recruited many disaffected anti-EU Conservatives. The party spent much of the '90s and early 2000s targeting southern Conservatives in the hope of converting them from 'soft' Euroscepticism (staying in the EU but agitating for reform), to its own 'hard' Euroscepticism (withdrawing from the EU altogether). But this no longer reflects the party's wider support base, or its strategy.

Since returning as leader after the 2010 general election, Farage has urged his party to 'gun for Labour'. This partly reflects UKIP's goal of forcing Ed Miliband and Labour to match David Cameron's promise of a referendum on Britain's EU membership, but also the party's awareness of its ability to poll strongly in Labour areas. In the 2014 European elections UKIP averaged over 40 per cent in areas like North East Lincolnshire and Rotherham. For some within the party, the best possible outcome of the 2015 general election is a fragile Labour government, enabling UKIP to cement its presence as the main opposition to Labour in some of its northern core seats by soaking up opposition to the government.

The party's emergence as a voice of the disaffected working class is not as surprising as it first appears. Elsewhere in Europe, more established radical right parties also nearly always draw their core support from disaffected, older and white working-class men. The radical right revolt in Britain is a late-starter but it is drawing its strength from the very same sections of society. UKIP's success in struggling post-industrial towns like Rotherham and Grimsby is mirrored by National Front success in similar rust belt French towns such as Hénin-Beaumont, a former socialist stronghold in the heart of former coal mining territory.

For a generation, British politicians on both the right and the left have followed the Blairite doctrine that they must project a professional, socially liberal and politically moderate image to win elections. Now their strongest new challenge in a generation is coming from a party which rejects all of this. Resolutely traditionalist, immoderate and amateurish, UKIP reject all of the rules of British politics, yet, like the proverbial bumblebee, still they fly. The sudden emergence of a band of gleeful, Brussels-bashing, working-class rebels onto the main stage of British politics is a sobering reminder that no political rule book is written in stone: politics is far too unpredictable for that. Those writing the next rule book might want to start with a close examination of the party which tore up the old one.

FURTHER READING

The most comprehensive examination of UKIP's electoral support is in Robert Ford and Matthew Goodwin's *Revolt on the Right: Explaining Support for the Radical Right in Britain* (Routledge, 2014). You can also learn more about Conservative voters who defect to UKIP in European Parliament elections in 'Strategic Eurosceptics and Polite Xenophobes: Support for the United Kingdom Independence Party in the 2009 European Parliament elections' by Robert Ford et al. (*European Journal of Political Research*, 2012). 'Euroscepticism and the Referendum Party' by Anthony Heath et al. (*British Elections and Parties Yearbook*, 1998) provides a good introduction to UKIP's political predecessor. Cas Mudde's *Populist Radical Right Parties in Europe* (Cambridge University Press, 2007) provides a wide-ranging introduction to the radical right family of parties which have appeared across Europe over the past few decades.

—CHAPTER 45—

Bedroom politics: party images

Joe Twyman

S ex and politics often go hand and hand. Although not all political
figures command the kind of animal magnetism of a Roy Hat-
tersley or an Ann Widdecombe, many have let their sexual desires
overcome them during the course of their political careers. Yet despite
sex being such an important part of political life, and life in general,
relatively little substantive research has been conducted in this area.

To get a sense of how different parties' supporters deviate, or not,
from the typical Briton, we first need a sense of what 'normal' looks
like. To do this, YouGov asked a nationally representative sample of
British adults to select words from a list which they felt most accurately described both the sexual behaviour and the sexual desires of
a typical British adult. Brits don't come out of it very well. Top of the
list of attributes used to describe their sex life was conventional (49
per cent), infrequent and short-lasting (both 30 per cent), and boring (28 per cent). Asked what they thought Britons liked to do during
sex, the top answers were: receiving oral sex (51 per cent), passionate kissing (40 per cent), and giving oral sex (29 per cent) – the last
ranking equally along with, curiously, sex with a work colleague.

This, then, is what the man and woman on the street thinks of as a typical British sex life. How do they imagine the sex lives of different parties' supporters compare to this average? The table identifies the areas in which the peccadilloes of partisans were perceived to be (statistically significantly) distinct from those of the average voter, giving the size of that difference in percentage points.

PUBLIC PERCEPTIONS ABOUT THE SEXUAL BEHAVIOUR AND DESIRES OF PARTY SUPPORTERS

TYPICAL SUPPORTER OF...	MOST OVER-REPRESENTED BEHAVIOURS	MOST UNDER-REPRESENTED BEHAVIOURS	MOST OVER-REPRESENTED DESIRES	MOST UNDER-REPRESENTED DESIRES
Conservatives	Dominant (+10) Boring (+10) Unusual (+6) Bad (+5)	Infrequent (-16) Lazy (-9) Short-lasting (-8) Varied (-8)	Sex with an MP (+31) Cross-dressing (+16) Spanking (+16) Blindfolds/bondage (both +11)	Receiving oral sex (-24) Sex with pop/rock star (-24) Passionate kissing (-24) Sex with TV/movie star (-21)
Labour	Rough (+15) Good (+7) Frequent (+6) Confident (+6)	Conventional (-23) Infrequent (-20) Shy (-9) Lazy/short lasting (-8)	Sex with an MP (+12) Sex with someone from different ethnic group (+10) Cross-dressing (+5)	Receiving oral sex (-25) Sex with pop/rock star (-18) Threesome (two women, one man) (-17) Sex with TV/movie star (-16)
Liberal Democrats	Boring (+16) Submissive (+16) Slow (+8) Gentle (+7)	Conventional (-18) Consistent (-12) Lazy (-11) Infrequent/fast (-9)	Sex with an MP (+26) Cross-dressing (+14) Homosexual sex (+11) Bondage (+10)	Receiving oral sex (-29) Passionate kissing (-25) Sex with pop/rock star (-22) Sex with TV/movie star (-17)
UKIP	Dominant (+20) Rough (+14) Bad (+14) Unusual (+7)	Conventional (-29) Infrequent (-16) Consistent (-14) Lazy/good (-10)	Sex with an MP (+15) Cross-dressing (+10) Sex with transsexual (+6) Receiving anal sex / bondage (both +5)	Passionate kissing (-27) Receiving oral sex (-26) Sex with pop/rock star (-21) Threesome (two women, one man)/wearing sexy outfit (both -18)

Source: YouGov

For example, the British public imagines Conservative supporters to be more likely to be dominant in bed than the typical Briton (by 10 percentage points). They also think of them as more likely to be boring (also ten points), unusual (six) and bad (five points). However, the good news for Conservatives is that they are at least seen as more likely to work hard: respondents expected more varied and long-lasting sex from Conservative supporters, who are also seen as less lazy and less likely to doom them to 'infrequent' conjugal encounters. Turn to desires, and the typical Conservative is expected to be quite sexually flamboyant: cross-dressing, spanking, wearing blindfolds and bondage are all perceived to be more prevalent among Conservative supporters (perhaps a legacy of the Major government, when some Conservative MPs publicly demonstrated an interest in any or all of these). The most widespread Tory desire, though, is believed to be sex with an MP. More conventional romantic activities such as receiving oral sex, sex with (non-political) celebrities or passionate kissing, are thought to be of less interest to Conservative partisans than the average voter.

How about Labour supporters? They are more likely to be seen as 'good' and 'confident' in the bedroom, highly active, and long-lasting. Dating Labour backers is not a game for the faint hearted, though, since they are also more likely to be described as 'rough' and 'dominant' in the bedroom and less likely to be seen as 'conventional'. Unlike Conservatives, Labour supporters are not seen as sexual fantasists: the only desires they are expected to go in for more than the average member of the public is sex with an MP and sex with someone from a different ethnic group. But like the Conservatives, Labour supporters are expected to be much less interested in the desires – oral sex, celebrities, threesomes and porn – which interest the average voter. The Labour man and woman in the bedroom is a paradox: confident, dominant but largely lacking in sexual imagination.

But supporters of both main parties can take some comfort from how their bedroom image compares with those of their smaller competitors. Liberal Democrat supporters are perceived to be boring, submissive, slow *and* inconsistent in the bedroom, although on the plus side they are also seen as gentle, and are less likely to be rated conventional and lazy. Like Conservative supporters, Lib Dems are perceived to have exotic sexual desires, centred on cross-dressing, gay sex, bondage and spanking, as well as the usual expectation – common to all parties – that party supporters want to bed MPs.

UKIP supporters are perceived as poor performers in the bedroom: dominant, rough, and bad, and less likely to be seen as conventional or consistent, although they are at least regarded to be keen on sex: 'infrequent' and 'lazy' are words the average person does not associate with UKIP sexual behaviour. UKIPers are also expected to have unusual desires, involving cross-dressing, receiving anal sex, bondage, sex with a transsexual and (yes, again) sex with an MP.

All good fun. Yet there are a couple of serious messages lodged in among all the kinky imagery. First, voters have quite distinctive views about the sex lives of Britain's main political tribes, illustrating the power of political stereotypes and party images, which reach even into the nation's bedrooms.

Second, while the parties have distinct bedroom images in the minds of voters, voters tend to regard all party supporters as deviating from the bedroom behaviour of 'normal' (that is, non-political) citizens. Politics is not seen as something normal people do: the evidence here underlines just how different – *weird*, even – those doing it are seen to be. It surely isn't entirely healthy for democracy if those who take to political battle with enthusiasm are regarded by the people who must vote for them as sexual oddballs.

FURTHER READING

There are some subjects where further reading should be undertaken with some caution. But for more on individuals' sexual fantasies, see Brett Kahr's *Sex and the Psyche: The Truth About Our Most Secret Fantasies* (Penguin, 2008), based on a large YouGov survey of 19,000 individuals. For a more orthodox treatment of the subject of party image, see Gary Davies and Takir Mian's 'The reputation of the party leader and of the party being led' (*European Journal of Marketing*, 2010).

—CHAPTER 46—

Liking Nigel makes you vote UKIP: party leader images and electoral choice

Harold Clarke

Party leaders are omnipresent figures in modern British politics. Followed incessantly by the press and appearing virtually every evening on television, they are, both literally and figuratively, the public faces of their parties. However, the straightforward conclusion that party leaders matter was long neglected by researchers who gave scant attention to the public's impressions of these political figures.

This neglect is puzzling because there is abundant empirical evidence that feelings about party leaders are influential when voters go to the polls. In recent years these findings have been given theoretical grounding in what is called the 'valence politics' account of the political psychology of electoral choice. This views leader images as cues ('heuristics' is the fancy term) that enable voters to make decisions in situations where stakes are high and uncertainty abounds. According to valence politics theory, voters are 'smart enough to know they are not smart enough'. Following the sage advice of 'Dirty Harry' Callahan, voters recognise their limitations and turn to readily available, low cost, cues provided by leaders (and parties) for assistance.

The influence of leader images on voting decisions is not confined to how people react to those at the helm of long-lived, major parties such as the Conservatives and Labour. Rather, it extends to leaders of minor parties, with the impact of Nigel Farage, leader of the United Kingdom Independence Party (UKIP), being a good example. Since the coalition government came to power in May 2010, UKIP has moved up smartly in the polls, with most analysts arguing that the party's surge has been propelled by a potent mixture of political alienation, hostility to the EU and anti-immigrant sentiments, combined with the Liberal Democrats' unavailability as a vehicle for voicing political protest. Yet, take all that into account, and feelings about Mr Farage still matter too.

Data in the graph are based on an analysis of national survey data gathered in January and February 2014. Consider someone we might expect to be tempted by UKIP: a sixty-year-old, middle-class man, say, living in Boxford, South Suffolk. Otherwise average in his political attitudes, this person does not have a sense of attachment to any of the parties, but has concluded that UKIP is best able to handle Britain's relations with the EU, the issue that matters most to him. Nevertheless, as the graph shows, the probability that he will support UKIP in the next general election varies greatly depending on how he feels about Nigel Farage. If the voter strongly dislikes Mr Farage, the probability of casting a UKIP ballot is merely 0.03 points on a 0–1 scale. However, as feelings about Farage become increasingly positive, this probability moves sharply upwards, reaching fully 0.82 points at the top end of the like-dislike scale. Liking Nigel greatly enhances the likelihood of voting for his party.

The pattern does not just apply to reactions to Mr Farage – widely reputed to be a convivial bloke with whom to down a pint. Similar findings obtain for voters' reactions to David Cameron, Ed Miliband,

Nick Clegg and all earlier party leaders for whom the requisite survey data are available. Clegg provides a good example. Consider the same hypothetical voter as the one described above, with the exception that this individual now believes that the Liberal Democrats are best able to articulate the case for continued British membership in the EU, the issue the voter considers most important. If this person strongly dislikes Mr Clegg, his probability of voting Liberal Democrat is only 0.04. However, that probability quickly climbs as feelings about Clegg become increasingly positive, reaching fully 0.88 points if the voter really likes the Liberal Democrat leader.

FEELINGS ABOUT NIGEL FARAGE AND PROBABILITY OF VOTING UKIP

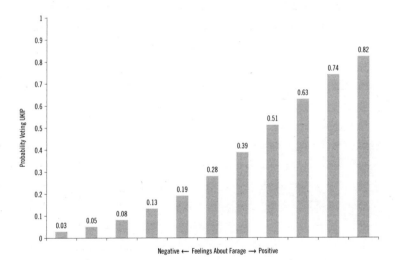

Why are feelings about the leaders consequential? Research indicates that the simple, but powerful, feelings of like and dislike voters form about various leaders conveniently encapsulate perceptions of these figures as (in)competent, (un)responsive, and (un)trustworthy. Quite simply, voters are a street-smart lot who rightly believe that leaders are important figures in British politics. Using readily available information to form summary impressions of the leaders gives voters a 'fast and frugal' heuristic to inform their electoral choices. Many psephologists now wisely recognise what most punters have long known: leaders matter.

FURTHER READING

Leader effects were reluctantly admitted (and minimised) in David Butler and Donald Stokes's *Political Choice in Britain* (St Martin's Press, 1969). The theory of valence politics emphasising the importance of party leader image and partisan heuristics is presented in *Political Choice and Britain* by Harold Clarke et al. (Oxford University Press, 2004) and, by the same authors, *Performance Politics and the British Voter* (Cambridge University Press, 2009). On the rise of UKIP see Chapters 6 and 9 of *Affluence, Austerity and Electoral Change in Britain* by Paul Whiteley et al. (Cambridge University Press, 2013) and Robert Ford and Matthew Goodwin's *Revolt on the Right: Explaining Support for the Radical Right in Britain* (Routledge, 2014).

—CHAPTER 47—

Leaders matters:
a tale of two
Labour Prime Ministers

Geoffrey Evans

The identification of 'leadership effects' is not straightforward. The connection between liking, say, David Cameron, and intending to vote for the Conservatives is rather obvious, but proves little. That popular parties have popular leaders (and vice versa) is not sufficient to demonstrate that leaders make the parties they lead popular. It could be the other way around or the popularity of both might result from something else.

As an example, take Gordon Brown. Many people have pointed to his evident shortcomings as party leader when explaining Labour's defeat in 2010. He is often compared, unflatteringly, with his predecessor, Tony Blair. But other candidate explanations for that defeat, which could have been far worse, are numerous: the global economic crisis, immigration policy, and the prolonged occupation of Afghanistan to name but three. Had Brown's succession to Blair not corresponded closely with the stalling of the housing market, the run on Northern Rock, the collapse of Lehman

Brothers, a descent into recession, a debt crisis, and rising immigration, then aggregate polls of the sort published in the press would provide enough insights to answer the question of which Labour leader was the biggest vote winner (or loser). But in reality, their party's electoral performance is too mixed up in all of these other factors for us to be able to tell.

Fortunately, detailed studies of leaders' evaluations have been undertaken which have followed the same individuals across the full electoral cycle – known as panel studies – which enable us to track the evolution of individual voters' decisions.

We can therefore examine the perceptions and motives of individual voters who left Labour and failed to come back, and attempt to take into account all the competing explanations for their eventual vote.

The figure compares the predicted likelihood of defection from supporting Labour as a result of feelings towards Blair in 2005–6 and Brown in 2009–10, once economic perceptions, immigration concerns, NHS worries, and a whole range of other factors had been taken into account.

Feelings towards the party leaders are measured by asking the following question: 'Using a scale that runs from 0 to 10, where 0 means strongly dislike and 10 means strongly like, how do you feel about (Tony Blair/Gordon Brown)?'

The dot indicates the likelihood of defection away from Labour, and the lines around the dot indicate the margin of error on each estimate.

THE EFFECT OF LEADER EVALUATIONS ON THE LIKELIHOOD OF DEFECTING FROM LABOUR IN 2005–6 (BLAIR) AND 2009–10 (BROWN)

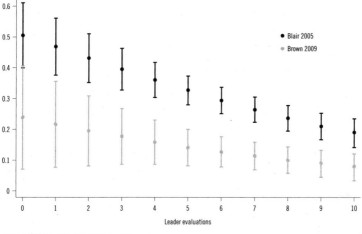

Source: BEPS 2005–2010, base: all Labour voters

Two things are apparent. The first is that the leadership effect is visibly stronger for Blair, with the probability of defection decreasing steeply from 51 per cent to 19 per cent along the feeling thermometer scale. Each point increase in feelings towards Blair substantially reduces the risk of defection away from Labour. For Brown, the risk of switching from Labour decreases too, but less sharply from 24 per cent to 8 per cent, and the effect is only statistically detectable at the higher values of the feeling thermometer (from seven onwards). Dislike of Blair would appear to be more decisive for Labour voters' defection in 2005–6, in the aftermath of the Iraq invasion, than aversion to Brown was in 2009–10, in the aftermath of the economic crisis.

The second striking feature of the graph is that for every position on the eleven-point scale, the chances of defecting from Labour were higher when Tony Blair was the leader than when Gordon Brown was leader. Both leaders were unpopular with voters in the periods under examination, and both were electoral liabilities rather than assets. However, Labour were in a stronger position when Blair faced the electorate in 2005 – at a time of economic growth and continued Conservative unpopularity – than Brown was five years later, in the aftermath of the financial crisis. Blair's unpopularity in 2005 was therefore more damaging to Labour because the party then still won a lot of support from swing voters who might be swayed by their views of the leader. Under Brown, Labour support had been cut to the bone, and the remaining tribal loyalists were less likely to switch simply because they didn't like Brown's leadership. In other words, the damage done by Brown has probably been exaggerated, and the damage done by Blair in his last campaign was probably worse than many people realise – if only because things were so bad for Labour already in 2010 that Brown's unpopularity could scarcely make them worse.

This is a useful reminder of how the effects of leaders are dependent on the context in which the party finds itself. We need to think a little more carefully about what sort of leader, what sort of party, and what sort of effect. Established parties have an element of entrenched support that can weaken the impact of a particular leader. But when a party has a low profile and little track record the leader might be their best bet. An exemplar of the latter is UKIP (see Chapter 46). Without Nigel Farage's 'man in the street' bonhomie – quite an achievement for a Dulwich public schoolboy who went on to become a City trader – UKIP would be a far less prominent player in the current electoral mix. Sometimes, perhaps, it might be better for parties if leaders kept their heads down and didn't matter quite so much. This might even be Ed Miliband's optimal strategy. Although he is unpopular, his opposite number is not well loved either, and he has a number of other factors in his favour. Sometimes leadership means getting out of the way.

FURTHER READING

For the view that parties not leaders matter see John Bartle and Ivor Crewe's 'The impact of party leaders in Britain' in *Leaders' Personalities and the Outcomes of Democratic Elections* (Oxford University Press, 2002). On how we can tell if Labour's leaders mattered in the various elections of the first decade of the century, see: Robert Andersen and Geoffrey Evans's 'Who Blairs wins? Leadership and voting in the 2001 election' (*Journal of Elections, Public Opinion and Parties*, 2003); 'The impact of party leadership on voting: How Blair lost Labour votes' by the same authors (*Parliamentary Affairs*, 2005); and Geoffrey Evans and Kat Chzhen's 'Explaining Voters' Defection from Labour over the 2005–2010 Electoral Cycle: Leaders, Economics, and the Rising Importance of Immigration' (*Political Studies*, 2013).

CHAPTER 48

Scarecrows or tin men: talking about party leaders

Kristi Winters

In late 2013 one British national newspaper ran the results of a survey that replicated a famous question first posed by the American pollster John Zogby: 'Imagine you live in the land of Oz, and the candidates are the Tin Man, who's all brains and no heart, and the Scarecrow, who's all heart and no brains. Who would you vote for?'

In addition to the overall result (41 per cent chose the Tin Man while 32 per cent went for the Scarecrow), the newspaper reported there were 'big differences in gender and region' and that women favoured the Scarecrow who was 'all heart, no brains' while men preferred the Tin Man's 'all brains, no heart'.

Closer inspection shows the results weren't quite that clear cut. Sure, 46 per cent of men chose the Tin Man while 27 per cent chose the Scarecrow, a nineteen point difference. But women did not have a clear preference: 37 per cent selected the Scarecrow and 36 per cent the Tin Man, a one point difference.

Recent qualitative electoral research suggests there are some limited differences in the way men and women evaluate leaders, but not for the sexual stereotypical reasons the newspaper headline suggests.

For example, focus group research from 2005 investigated whether men and women have distinct frameworks for evaluating party leaders. Those results indicated that men and women used the same categories to discuss candidates: leadership qualities, personality assessments and trustworthiness. Men and women rated Prime Minister Tony Blair as a strong leader despite many negative assessments of his (post-Iraq War) trustworthiness and personality. Conservative Party leader Michael Howard received negative assessments on his leadership, trustworthiness and personality from men and women. The only sex difference was found in the evaluations of Liberal Democrat leader Charles Kennedy: while everyone saw him as trustworthy, women mentioned his good personal qualities but men focused on his lack of political weight.

In 2010 three leaders' debate night focus groups with twenty-three people (twelve women and eleven men) looked at photos of Gordon Brown, David Cameron and Nick Clegg. Respondents were asked to write down the words that came to mind for each man. Here are a few examples of participants assessing their leadership, personality and trustworthiness.

Leadership:
Deborah: I hate to say it but I think ... Gordon Brown's fail to lead his own government and his own party so I put him at the bottom, but actually I think that I would put David Cameron at the top and Nick Clegg below which is not – which is contrary to my personal political beliefs – but I think ... that he [Cameron] seems to be more the leader of his party, bearing in mind that

particularly Nick Clegg has Vince ... whereas David Cameron's come in and really seems to have taken control in quite a strong way.

Personality:

Keith: I put that he's 'caring' in certain things. I think he [Brown] does care. Whether he does it in the right way or not, I don't know.

Trustworthiness:

Cathy: I put 'genuine demeanour' for some reason, he [Clegg] looked a bit more genuine in that picture.

If you organise all the comments into the categories of Leader, Personality and Trust and compare the responses you find a subtle sex difference in leadership evaluations that mirrors men and women's responses to the Scarecrow v. Tin Man question (reported in the table). Men in the focus groups wrote more words that evaluated the leadership qualities for the three main party leaders: 63 per cent of the forty-six words were coded as evaluating Brown's leadership, 43 per cent for Cameron and 70 per cent for Clegg.

Women, however, were more evenly split between leadership assessments and personal assessments: 38 per cent leadership compared to 45 per cent on the personal for Brown, 36 per cent leader to 38 per cent for Cameron, and the one instance where leadership was the most common assessment: Clegg with 51 per cent of the words relating to his leadership and 34 per cent on the personal. (These mentions include positive, negative and neutral comments, and for Clegg many respondents wrote words or phrases to indicate they didn't know much about him; these were coded as leadership mentions.)

PERCENTAGE OF WORDS WRITTEN BY LEADERSHIP CATEGORY AND BY SEX

GORDON BROWN	LEADER	PERSONAL	TRUST	TOTAL
Women	38	45	17	100
Men	63	28	9	100

DAVID CAMERON	LEADER	PERSONAL	TRUST	TOTAL
Women	36	38	26	100
Men	43	26	31	100

NICK CLEGG	LEADER	PERSONAL	TRUST	TOTAL
Women	51	34	15	100
Men	70	19	11	100

Source: Qualitative Election Study of Britain 2010
N words by sex = Brown: 60 (women) 46 (men), Cameron N = 50 (women) 42 (men), Clegg N = 41 (women) 37 (men)

This evidence suggests men and women assess leaders using the same categories but they don't apply them with the same frequency. Men in our focus groups looked at and assessed the candidates most often on a leadership quality while women reacted more holistically to the candidate as a person. It is not that women favour 'all heart, no brains' while men preferred 'all brains, no heart', but rather that men focus more heavily on 'brains' while women give equal weight to 'brains' and 'heart'.

Voters' decisions are rarely as simple as newspaper headlines would like them to be. People's evaluations of party leaders are complicated, bound up with their own party identification, economic considerations on both a personal and national level along with other factors. When examined up close, the political similarities and differences between men and women are far more interesting than the one-dimensional gender stereotypes presented in the media.

FURTHER READING

The 2005 focus group research can be found in Kristi Winters and Rosie Camp-bell's 'Hearts or Minds: Men, Women and Leader Evaluations in the 2005 General Election' in *Political Communications: The General Election Campaign of 2005* (Pal-grave Macmillan, 2007). Results of the 2010 focus groups were published by Kristi Winters and Edzia Carvalho in '2010 British General Election Leader Evaluations: Replicating Electoral Focus Group Research' (*The Qualitative Report*, 2013). Zogby's question is explained in his *The Way We'll Be* (Random House, 2009), and its Brit-ish usage was reported in 'Who should run Britain: Tin Man Cameron (all head, no heart) or Scarecrow Miliband (all heart, no brains), asks Wizard of Oz poll' (*Daily Mail*, 3 December 2013).

—CHAPTER 49—

From Churchill to a Nazi: party leaders and the press

Daniel Stevens

A study of the content of newspapers in the 2010 election revealed that stories about leaders, their integrity, and the televised debates between them dwarfed coverage of issues such as the economy, education, and the NHS, and was only outweighed by coverage of the horserace – the state of the polls, campaign strategies and so on – which itself often segues into discussion of leaders. It is also overwhelmingly the leaders' voices that we hear in press discussion of politics: when we read stories that referred to or quoted someone from one of the three major parties, in about seven out of ten of cases that individual was Brown, Cameron or Clegg. Even in 2001 and 2005, and without the excuse of the leaders' debates, the equivalent figure was around 50 per cent. But does press coverage like this matter? Does all of this coverage influence the way voters feel about the party leaders?

There are some major challenges in answering these sorts of questions: readers choose newspapers that reflect their political views, rather than taking their political views from the papers they read; coverage may move some readers in one direction but move others in the opposite direction so that even if lots of people have been influenced the net effect may appear to be zero; and there's the fact that effects on outcomes via perceptions of leaders are indirect – one must first gauge the impact of press coverage on perceptions of leaders and then the impact of perceptions of leaders on voting behaviour, which can be doubly difficult.

It is also hard to get data to test these questions. The 2010 British Election Study indicated that about three-quarters of the public read a daily newspaper or followed news on the internet. It would be useful to have studies that linked such coverage over long periods of time to these readers' perceptions of leaders but we lack such detailed evidence on the ebb and flow of readers' opinions. We are thus dependent on data drawn from election periods, meaning the question becomes a narrower one: what the effects of the press coverage of leaders are over the four to six weeks of a general election campaign. By its very nature, this is an abbreviated period during which changes are less likely to occur.

While *The Sun* was quick to claim that its front page story with Neil Kinnock's head in a light bulb was 'wot won it' for the Conservatives in 1992 the reality is that headlines on the day of voting do not change election outcomes. Indeed, if the criterion is that for press coverage of leaders to matter it must be *the* decisive factor in how people vote then it probably does not matter – but then nor does much else in elections. Nevertheless, media coverage of leaders does still appear to have some net impact. For example, the focus on aspects of leaders' personalities and characters can lead voters to weight such traits more heavily. In 2005 campaign coverage of Tony Blair elevated his trustworthiness (or lack of it) into a central political question. Voters responded by weighting Blair's trustworthiness more heavily in their evaluations: at the beginning of the campaign trusting or not trusting Blair resulted in a difference of about three points on a ten-point scale asking how much they liked him; but by the end of the campaign this had increased to about 4.5 among newspaper readers. This translates, in turn, to a difference in the probability of voting Labour of more than 25 per cent.

We see the same kinds of effects with the issues the press focuses upon. Take Iraq in 2005. Heightened coverage of the war in the press during the election campaign encouraged people to link their political choices to their views of the war: the difference this issue made in like-dislike of Tony Blair increased from 2.5 points to 3.5 points, translating to a difference in the probability of voting Labour of about 20 per cent. In other words, in terms of its impact on evaluations of leaders, it is not so much what the press tells readers to think as what the press tells readers to think *about* that matters. In 2010, Nick Clegg complained that coverage had changed from characterising him as Churchill to a Nazi in a week. Did it matter? Attacks on Clegg's character were especially prevalent in the 'Tory press', some of whose readers were in fact Liberal Democrats (15 to 20 per cent for newspapers like the *Daily Telegraph*, *Daily Express* and *Daily Mail*). Readers of Conservative newspapers were particularly likely to be swayed in their evaluations of Clegg by whether or not they regarded him as having 'your best interests in mind', something that they were unlikely to have associated with Nazi sympathies. Indeed, the evidence suggests that viewing Clegg as most unlikely to have your best interests in mind lessened the probability of voting Liberal Democrat by about 15 per cent. Did David Cameron also benefit from a supportive Tory press? To an extent, yes. Simply reading a Conservative newspaper, accounting for all kinds of other factors such as someone's Conservative inclinations to begin with, led to higher evaluations of Cameron and a boost in the probability of voting Conservative of about 3 per cent. But reading a Conservative newspaper also enhanced the influence of agreeing that Cameron 'knows what he is talking about', the attribute on which he was rated most positively at the outset of the campaign, and on which he was rated more positively than the other two major party leaders. Ultimately this made a difference of about 12 per cent in the probability of a reader of a Conservative newspaper actually voting Conservative.

In 2015, we should look for the Conservatives and the Conservative press to emphasise character issues such Cameron's competence and knowledge as Prime Minister over Ed Miliband's more uncertain reputation and for Miliband to try to emphasise his advantage of being seen to be closer to the concerns of ordinary voters, though without the widespread press support enjoyed by his rival (or his predecessor, Blair, in 1997). If newspapers continue to focus on leaders 70 per cent of the time then this battle to frame perceptions in the media will have a real impact on the election outcome.

FURTHER READING

The research on coverage of character and Iraq in the 2005 election mentioned above can be found in Daniel Stevens and Jeffrey Karp's 'Leadership Traits and Media Influence in Britain' (*Political Studies*, 2012) and 'Priming Time for Blair? Media Priming, Iraq, and Leadership Evaluations in Britain' by Daniel Stevens et al. (*Electoral Studies*, 2011). An enlightening look at changing media norms of coverage is Ana Ines Langer's *The Personalisation of Politics in the UK: Mediated Leadership from Attlee to Cameron* (Manchester University Press, 2012).

'But this is terrible – they've elected a Labour government and the country will never stand for that!'

UNIDENTIFIED (AND POSSIBLY APOCRYPHAL)
LADY DINER IN THE SAVOY HOTEL, 26 JULY 1945

—CHAPTER 50—

Iain Dale, naked:
exit polls

John Curtice

'It seems too incredible to be true that the Lib Dems are only predicted to get fifty-nine seats. I'll run naked down Whitehall if that turns out to be true.'

So wrote Iain Dale, onetime political blogger and Tory candidate now turned well known radio host and book publisher, on the night of 6 May 2010. The three main broadcasting organisations, BBC, ITV and Sky, had just published the results of the exit poll they had jointly commissioned estimating how people had voted in the general election. After an election campaign that had seen a dramatic if gradually fading bounce in the Liberal Democrats' poll ratings, the poll had predicted that the party would win just fifty-nine seats, four fewer than they had secured in 2005. In the event they actually won just fifty-seven.

Was not Mr Dale's scepticism understandable? After all, had not the exit polls, along with everyone else, forecast that Labour would win in 1992, when in the event the Conservatives were re-elected with a majority of twenty-one seats? Does not the intelligent commentator treat an exercise that can make an error as monumental as that with a very large pinch of salt?

Well, just to set the record straight, the exit polls did not forecast that Labour would win in 1992. They correctly suggested (unlike most regular opinion polls) that the Tories would be the largest party – they 'just' failed to identify the fact that they were on course to win an overall majority. Meanwhile, one might equally recall the forecast of the 2005 exit poll: a Labour majority of sixty-six seats, which proved to be exactly in line with what transpired and which was rather less than many people had been anticipating. If the exit poll had correctly confounded expectations once before then maybe it would do so again?

Still, we are getting ahead of ourselves. What is an exit poll? It is an exercise in which people are approached as they leave a sample of polling stations across the country and are asked to complete a mock ballot paper to indicate how they have just voted. The results are then collated and analysed with a view to predicting at 10pm – when the polling stations close – what the overall outcome in seats will be. It provides those who do not wish to wait up all night with an indication of the news to which they are likely to wake up in the morning, while insomniac journalists and politicians acquire some advance intelligence of the parliamentary arithmetic with which they are going to have to wrestle in a few hours' time.

This sounds like a very easy exercise. Ask voters how they have voted, add up the totals for each party, and then work out how many seats each party is likely to obtain as a result.

In practice it is far from an easy undertaking on which to embark. For a start no organisation can afford to cover all of the 40,000 or so polling stations at which people vote. They have to select a small sample of stations at which to conduct their interviews. However, unlike in most other countries, in the UK general elections are not counted, and the results are not published, polling station by polling station. Consequently it is virtually impossible to know whether or not any particular sample of polling stations is in fact likely to reflect the behaviour of the country as a whole.

Exit polls have therefore given up trying to find such a set of stations. Instead, the approach nowadays is based on the observation that although the level of support for each political party varies considerably from one constituency to another, the extent to which the *change* in a party's level of support varies from one seat to another is much less, and is thus more likely to be estimated correctly by any set of polling stations. Thus rather than attempting to estimate each party's share of the vote, the exit poll attempts to estimate how much each party's vote is up or down since the last election and then applies those estimates to the actual result last time.

But how can that possibly be done if we do not know the result in each polling station last time around? Well, the one set of polling stations for which we do have an estimate of how people voted last time are the stations at which an exit poll was conducted last time around. So if, wherever possible, the exit poll is conducted at exactly the same places as last time, we can derive an estimate of how much each party's vote is up or down by comparing the tally of votes for each party this time with the equivalent tally last time.

There are though a couple of other crucial stages to the process. First, a party's support may systematically go up or down rather more in certain kinds of constituencies than in others. That could have an impact on how many seats it looks likely to win (because, for example, it means its vote is holding up better or worse in marginal seats). The exit poll analysts thus have to try to identify any evidence of systematic variation in how much each party's vote is changing, and, if necessary, produce different estimates of change for different kinds of constituencies.

Second, we should bear in mind that our estimate of how much each party's vote will rise or fall in each constituency is subject to sampling error. So if we estimate that two parties are in a close race for first place, we should be wary of assuming that whichever party is expected to be (narrowly) ahead will definitely win the seat. It is more realistic to say that both parties have a 50 per cent or so chance of winning. Consequently, for each party an estimate is derived of the probability that they will win each of the 633 seats in Great Britain; the total number of seats a party is forecast to win is then the sum of those probabilities across all seats. This feature proved especially crucial in enabling the poll to produce an accurate estimate of Labour's majority in 2005: there were lots of seats where the party was only just the favourite to come first, many of which it subsequently failed to win.

Even then, there are still plenty of risks. Not all voters are willing to take part in exit polls, and the results will be skewed if one party's supporters are more reluctant to do so than those of others. Sometimes the geographical area served by a polling station is changed, making it impossible to compare the result this time with last time. Around 15 per cent of British voters vote by post rather than go to a polling station, and they could possibly behave differently. Meanwhile, most voters vote in the early evening of polling day, leaving very little time to analyse and spot the crucial patterns in the data. Nevertheless, the 2010 exit poll proved to be as successful as its predecessor five years earlier. As well as anticipating a fall in the number of Liberal Democrat seats, it predicted that the Conservatives would be the largest party with 307 seats, exactly in line with the eventual result.

We are still waiting for Mr Dale to keep his promise. But on second thoughts … let us see how good the exit poll is in 2015!

FURTHER READING

Full details of the method and accuracy of the 2005 exit poll are to be found in John Curtice and David Firth's 'Exit Polling in a Cold Climate: the BBC–ITV Experience in 2005 (with discussion)' (*Journal of the Royal Statistical Society Series A*, 2008). An equivalent analysis and description of the 2010 poll is to be found in 'Confounding the Commentators: How the 2010 Exit Poll got it (more or less) right' by John Curtice et al. (*Journal of Elections, Public Opinion and Parties*, 2011). For a history of exit polls and similar exercises in Britain before 2005, see Clive Payne's 'Election forecasting in the UK: The BBC's experience' (*EurAmerica*, 2003).

*'I don't know the question,
but sex is definitely the answer.'*

WOODY ALLEN

CHAPTER 51

More sex: party supporters between the sheets

Bernadeta Wilk

Politics divides us more than we realise. A considerable body of research has shown cultural differences between conservatives and liberals that extend way beyond their politics: what they eat and drink, what sort of jokes they like, what sort of art and music they like, what sort of cars they drive. One study even showed differences in how tidy their bedrooms are.

And it is not just the tidiness of bedrooms that reveals political divides, but what we do in them. A nationally representative sample of British adults was asked about their own sexual behaviour and fantasies in a YouGov poll. In each case this was then cross-referenced against their party support. The different demographic profile of each party's supporters means it is necessary to control for the age, gender, marital status and sexual orientation of respondents in order to identify the differences that are genuinely down to political allegiance rather than social background. The table therefore highlights the behaviour and fantasies which are more frequently, and less frequently, reported by each party's supporters once these things have been controlled for.

The table reveals a sharp divide between the parties usually considered of the 'right' and those of the 'left'.

Conservative supporters' bedroom lives are, well, conservative. They are more likely to describe their sexual behaviour as 'consistent' and 'conventional', and less likely to report fantasising about, or taking part in, a wide range of more exotic sexual behaviour. Conservatives are confident about their bedroom prowess, promising more frequent sex than others, and less shyness. While the public expected all party supporters to be more interested in sex with an MP (see Chapter 45), Conservative supporters are the only ones to actually report bedding politicians more than average. They are also more likely than other respondents to report fantasising about sex with a sports star.

Supporters of UKIP, the new kids on the right-wing block, are if anything even more conventional: they are more likely to describe themselves as lazy, and definitely not 'exciting', in the bedroom; they avoid sex with younger partners (which, for most UKIP supporters, rules out a lot of people) and their principal sexual fetish – in fantasy and reality – is the vibrator. The sexual reports of left-wing partisans, though, are quite different.

Labour partisans have high opinions of themselves in the bedroom: they are more likely to report long lasting, exciting and varied sex, and less likely to report being 'fast'. Labour supporters are also more experimental, in both fantasy and behaviour. They are more likely to report a wide range of fantasies, including outdoor sex, sex with someone else's partner, spanking and role play. Some fantasies – such as passionate kissing and sex with a stranger – attract Labour supporters but repel Conservative supporters, and there are no fantasies that are over-reported by both parties' supporters. Labour supporters' sexual behaviour is also more experimental – they are more likely than the average voter to have engaged in threesomes and bondage, and to have flings with sports stars, TV stars and older partners, while only MPs turn Tory voters' heads.

It is often alleged that Liberal Democrat supporters are unhappy about the coalition with the Conservatives, which was a marriage of necessity, and would be more comfortable in a partnership with Labour. The evidence on the sexual behaviour and fantasies of the three parties suggest there may be something in this. Like Labour supporters, Liberal Democrat partisans are often imaginative and experimental in the bedroom. Indeed, an even wider range of sexual behaviours are over-reported by Liberal Democrat backers than Labour partisans, including erotic massage, orgies, sex with someone from a different ethnicity and sex with a transsexual. Lib Dem fantasies also tend in exotic directions, featuring bondage, sex on film and watching others.

If the left–right divide in the bedroom is between more conventional and conservative behaviour between the sheets, and more experimental and diverse behaviour, then the Lib Dems certainly join Labour on the left.

BEHAVIOUR AND FANTASIES OF PARTY SUPPORTERS

SUPPORTER OF...	CONSERVATIVES	LABOUR	LIBERAL DEMOCRATS	UKIP
Over-represented self descriptions	Consistent, conventional, frequent	Long lasting, exciting, varied	Good, fast, shy	Lazy
Over-represented behaviour	Sex with an MP	Sex with someone significantly older, with a TV/movie star, with a sports star, threesome, bondage	Sex with someone of different ethnicity, passionate kissing, erotic massage, taking part in an orgy, watching others have sex, sex with a transsexual	Using a vibrator or dildo
Under-represented self-descriptions	Shy	Fast	Frequent	Exciting

SUPPORTER OF...	CONSERVATIVES	LABOUR	LIBERAL DEMOCRATS	UKIP
Under-represented behaviour	Sex with someone significantly older, of different ethnicity or someone else's partner, threesome (two men, one woman), using vibrator/dildo, watching someone masturbate, wearing sexy outfit, watching others have sex	Nothing	Nothing	Sex with someone significantly younger
Over-represented fantasies	Sex with a sports star	Sex outdoors, with a stranger, with a TV/movie star, with someone else's partner, oral sex (giving and receiving), passionate kissing, role play, spanking, wearing sexy outfits	Sex with someone of different ethnicity, watching someone masturbate, bondage, filming self having sex, sex with a transsexual	Using a vibrator or dildo
Under-represented fantasies	Passionate kissing, threesome, spanking, taking part in an orgy, threesome (two men, one woman), sex with someone of different ethnicity, sex with a stranger	Nothing	Nothing	Nothing

Source: YouGov

What all this highlights is that the differences which draw people into rival political camps stretch far beyond politics. No one is arguing that voters are more or less likely to be attracted to the parties as a result of this behaviour – do not expect slogans such as 'Vote Conservative. We're less likely to be keen on spanking' – but the differences in personality, values and outlook expressed in politics are also found in many other parts of life, including the bedroom. Voters who prefer a stable and orderly life appear to lean towards conventional sex and Conservative politics; those who embrace the new and unconventional may be more attracted to aspects of left-wing politics as well as to sexual experimentation. Political divides don't just reflect narrow differences of opinion about health policy or the deficit; they are also expressions of personality and outlook. Think carefully before talking politics when out on a date: you may be revealing more about yourself than you realise.

FURTHER READING

Predisposed by John R. Hibbing et al. (Routledge, 2014) is an excellent introduction to the field of non-political partisan differences. Of the hundreds of more detailed studies, see for example Glenn D. Wilson's 'Ideology and Humor Preferences' (*International Political Science Review*, 1990) and his 'Conservatism and Art Preferences' (*Journal of Personality and Social Psychology*, 1973). Tidy bedrooms (and offices) are examined in 'The Secret Lives of Liberals and Conservatives: Personality Profiles, Interaction Styles and the Things They Leave Behind' by Dana R. Carney et al. (*Political Psychology*, 2008).

Bibliography

Almond, Gabriel and Verba, Sidney, *The Civic Culture* (Princeton: Princeton University Press, 1963)

Andersen, Robert and Evans, Geoffrey, 'Who Blairs wins? Leadership and voting in the 2001 election', *Journal of Elections, Public Opinion and Parties* (2003), vol. 13, pp. 229–47

Ariely, Dan, *The (Honest) Truth About Dishonesty* (London: Harper Collins, 2012)

Arzheimer, Kai and Evans, Jocelyn, 'Geolocation and voting: Candidate-voter distance effects on party choice in the 2010 UK general election in England', *Political Geography* (2012), vol. 31, no. 5, pp. 301–310

Ashe, Jeanette, Campbell, Rosie, Childs, Sarah and Evans, Elizabeth, 'Stand by your man: women's political recruitment at the 2010 general election', *British Politics* (2010), vol. 5, no. 4, pp. 455–80

Banducci, Susan, Karp, Jeffrey, Thrasher, Michael and Rallings, Collin, 'Ballot Photographs as Cues in Low-Information Elections', *Political Psychology* (2008), vol. 29, no. 6, pp. 903–917

Bar, Moshe, Neta, Maital and Linz, Heather, 'Very First Impressions', *Emotion* (2006), vol. 6, no. 2, pp. 269–78

Bartle, John and Crewe, Ivor, 'The impact of party leaders in Britain', in King, Anthony (ed.), *Leaders' Personalities and the Outcomes of Democratic Elections* (Oxford: Oxford University Press, 2002), pp. 70–95

Baughman, John, 'Party, constituency, and representation: Votes on abortion in the British House of Commons', *Public Choice* (2004), vol. 120, no. 1-2, pp. 63–85

Bhatti, Yosef and Hansen, Kasper, 'Retiring from Voting: Turnout among Senior Voters', *Journal of Elections, Public Opinion and Parties* (2012), vol. 22, no.4, pp. 479–500

Bishop, George F., Oldendick, Robert W., Tuchfarber, Alfred J. and Bennett, Stephen E., 'Pseudo-Opinions on Public Affairs', *Public Opinion Quarterly* (1980), vol. 44, no. 2, pp. 198–209

Bishop, George F., *The Illusion of Public Opinion: Fact and Artifact in American Public Opinion Polls* (Oxford: Rowman & Littlefield, 2005)

Blinder, Scott, Ford, Robert, and Ivarsflaten, Elisabeth, 'The Better Angels of Our Nature: How the Antiprejudice Norm Affects Policy and Party Preferences in Great Britain and Germany', *American Journal of Political Science* (2013), vol. 57, no. 4, pp. 841–57

Bochel, J. M. and Denver, D. T., 'Canvassing, Turnout and Party Support: An Experiment', *British Journal of Political Science* (1971), vol. 1, no. 3, pp. 257–69

Butler, David and Stokes, Donald, *Political Choice in Britain* (New York: St. Martin's Press, 1969)

— —, *Political Change in Britain* (London: Macmillan, 1974)

Cain, Bruce, Ferejohn, John and Fiorina, Morris, *The Personal Vote: Constituency Service and Electoral Independence* (London: Harvard University Press, 1987)

Campbell, David E., *Why We Vote* (Princeton, New Jersey: Princeton University Press, 2006)

Campbell, Rosie 'What do we really know about women voters? Gender, elections and public opinion', *Political Quarterly* (2012), vol. 83, no. 4, pp. 703–710

— —, *Gender and the Vote in Britain* (Colchester, Essex: ECPR Press, 2006)

Campbell, Rosie and Cowley, Philip, 'What voters want: reactions to candidate characteristics in a survey experiment', *Political Studies* (2013) [Early View]

Campbell, Rosie and Lovenduski, Joni, 'Who knows what makes a good MP? Public and Parliamentarians' views compared', *Parliamentary Affairs* (forthcoming)

Carman, Christopher, Johns, Robert and Mitchell, James, *More Scottish than*

British? The 2011 Scottish Parliament Election (Basingstoke: Palgrave, 2014)

Carney, Dana R., Jost, John T., Gosling, Samuel D. and Potter, Jeff, 'The Secret Lives of Liberals and Conservatives: Personality Profiles, Interaction Styles and the Things They Leave Behind', *Political Psychology* (2008), vol. 29, no. 6, pp. 807–840

Chan, Tak Wing and Clayton, Matthew, 'Should the voting age be lowered to sixteen?', *Political Studies* (2006), vol. 54, no. 3, pp. 533–58

Childs, Sarah and Webb, Paul, *Sex, Gender and the Conservative Party* (Basingstoke: Palgrave, 2011)

Clark, Alistair, 'Second Time Lucky? The Continuing Adaptation of Parties and Voters to the Single Transferable Vote in Scotland', *Representation* (2013), vol. 49, no. 1, pp. 55–68

Clarke, Harold, Sanders, David, Stewart, Marianne C. and Whiteley, Paul, *Political Choice and Britain* (Oxford: Oxford University Press, 2004)

— —, 'Taking the bloom off New Labour's rose: party choice and voter turnout in Britain, 2005', *Journal of Elections, Public Opinion and Parties* (2006), vol. 16, no. 1, pp. 3–36

— —, *Performance Politics and the British Voter* (Cambridge: Cambridge University Press, 2009)

Converse, Philip, 'The nature of belief systems in mass publics', in Apter, David E. (ed.), *Ideology and Discontent* (New York Free Press of Glencoe, 1964), pp. 47–76

Cowley, Philip, 'Why not ask the audience? Understanding the public's representational priorities', *British Politics* (2013), vol. 8, pp. 138–63

— —, 'Descriptive representation and political trust: a quasi-natural experiment utilising ignorance', *Journal of Legislative Studies* (2014)

Criddle, Byron, 'More Diverse yet More Uniform', in Kavanagh, Dennis and Cowley, Philip *The British General Election 2010* (London: Palgrave Macmillan, 2010), pp. 306–329

Crossman, Richard, *The Diaries of A Cabinet Minister* (BCA, 1975–77)

Curtice, John, 'One Nation Again', *British Social Attitudes* (1996), vol. 13, pp. 1–17

Curtice, John and Firth, David, 'Exit Polling in a Cold Climate: the BBC-ITV Experience in 2005 (with discussion)', *Journal of the Royal Statistical Society Series A* (2008), vol. 171, no. 3, pp. 509–39

Curtice, John, Fisher, Stephen D. and Kuhai, Jouni, 'Confounding the Commentators: How the 2010 Exit Poll got it (more or less) right', *Journal of Elections, Public Opinion and Parties* (2011), vol. 21, no. 2, pp. 211–35

Curtice, John, McCrone, David, McEwen, Nicola, Marsh, Michael and Ormston, Rachel, *Revolution or Evolution? The 2007 Scottish Elections* (Edinburgh: Edinburgh University Press, 2009)

Curtice, John and Park, Alison, 'Region: New Labour, new geography?' in Evans, Geoffrey and Norris, Pippa, (eds) *Critical Elections: British Parties and Voters in Long-Term Perspective* (London: Sage, 1999), pp. 124–47

Cutts, David, 'Local Elections as a "Stepping Stone": Does Winning Council Seats Boost the Liberal Democrats' Performance in General Elections?', *Political Studies* (2014), vol. 62, no. 2, pp. 361–80

Cutts, David, Childs, Sarah and Fieldhouse, Edward, 'This is What Happens When You Don't Listen: All-Women Shortlists at the 2005 General Election', *Party Politics* (2008), vol. 14, no. 5, pp. 575–95

Cutts, David and Fieldhouse, Edward, 'What Small Spatial Scales Are Relevant as Electoral Contexts for Individual Voters? The Importance of the Household on Turnout at the 2001 General Election', *American Journal of Political Science* (2009), vol. 53, no.3, pp. 726–39

Cutts, David, Johnston, Ron, Pattie, Charles and Fisher, Justin, 'Laying the foundations for electoral success: Conservative pre-campaign canvassing before the 2010 general election', *Journal of Elections, Public Opinion and Parties* (2012), vol. 22, no. 3, pp. 359–75

Darnton, Andrew and Kirk, Martin, 'Finding Frames' [http://findingframes.org/report.htm] (2011)

Davies, Gary and Mian, Takir, 'The reputation of the party leader and of the party being led', *European Journal of Marketing* (2010), vol. 44, no. 3/4, pp.

331–50

De Rooij, Eline, Green, Donald P. and Gerber, Alan S., 'Field Experiments on Political Behavior and Collective Action', *Annual Review of Political Science* (2009), vol. 12, pp. 389–95

Denver, David, 'Another Reason to Support Marriage? Turnout and the Decline of Marriage in Britain', *British Journal of Politics and International Relations* (2008), vol. 10, no. 4, pp. 666–80

Denver, David, Clark, Alistair and Bennie, Lynn, 'Voter Reactions to a Preferential Ballot: The 2007 Scottish Local Elections', *Journal of Elections, Public Opinion and Parties* (2009), vol. 19, no. 3, pp. 265–82

Denver, David and Hands, Gordon, *Modern Constituency Electioneering* (London: Frank Cass, 1997).

Dorling, Danny, 'It is necessarily so', *Significance Magazine* (2013), vol. 10, no. 2, pp. 37–39

— —, 'Tolerance, inequality and the recession' *Sheffield Political Economy Research Institute Blog*, 1 March 2013

Duch, Ray and Stevenson, Randolph, *The Economic Vote: How Political and Economic Institutions Condition Election Results* (New York: Cambridge University Press, 2008)

Erikson, Robert, Mackuen, Michael B. and Stimson, James A., *The Macro Polity* (Cambridge: Cambridge University Press, 2002)

Evans, Elizabeth, *Gender and the Liberal Democrats* (Manchester: Manchester University Press, 2011)

Evans, Geoffrey and Andersen, Robert, 'The impact of party leadership on voting: How Blair lost Labour votes', *Parliamentary Affairs* (2005), vol. 58, no. 4, pp. 818–36

Evans, Geoffrey and Chzhen, Kat, 'Explaining Voters' Defection from Labour over the 2005–2010 Electoral Cycle: Leaders, Economics, and the Rising Importance of Immigration', *Political Studies* (2013), vol. 61, no. S1, pp. 3–22

Evans, Geoffrey and Tilley, James, 'How parties shape class politics: Structural transformation, ideological convergence and the decline of class voting in

Britain', *British Journal of Political Science* (2012), vol. 42, no. 1, pp. 137–61

— —, 'The depoliticization of inequality and redistribution: Explaining the decline of class voting', *Journal of Politics* (2012), vol. 74, no. 4, pp. 963–76

Evans, Geoffrey and Pickup, Mark, 'Reversing the Causal Arrow: The Political Conditioning of Economic Perceptions in the 2000–2004 U.S. Presidential Election Cycle', *Journal of Politics* (2010), vol. 72, no. 4, pp. 1236–51

Evans, Jocelyn and Tonge, Jon, 'Social Class and Party Choice in Northern Ireland's Ethnic Blocs', *West European Politics* (2009), vol. 32, no. 5, pp. 1012-30

— —, 'Northern Ireland' in Geddes, Andrew and Tonge, Jon, (eds) *Britain Votes 2010* (Oxford: Oxford University Press, 2010), pp. 158–75

Fieldhouse, Edward and Cutts, David, 'The Companion Effect: Household and Local Context and the Turnout of Young People', *Journal of Politics* (2012), vol. 74, no. 3, pp. 856–69

Fisher, Justin, 'Party Expenditure and Electoral Prospects: A National Level Analysis of Britain', *Electoral Studies* (1999), vol. 18, no. 4, pp. 519–32

— —, 'Party Finance – Normal Service Resumed?', *Parliamentary Affairs* (2010), vol. 63, no. 4, pp. 778–801

Fisher, Justin, Cutts, David and Fieldhouse, Edward, 'The electoral effectiveness of constituency campaigning in the 2010 British general election: The "triumph" of Labour', *Electoral Studies* (2011), vol. 30, no. 4, pp. 816–28

Fisher, Justin, Johnston, Ron, Cutts, David, Pattie, Charles and Fieldhouse, Edward, 'You get what you (don't) pay for: The impact of volunteer labour and candidate spending at the 2010 British General Election', *Parliamentary Affairs* (2014) [Available early online]

Fisher, Stephen D., 'Definition and measurement of tactical voting: The role of rational choice', *British Journal of Political Science* (2004), vol. 34, no. 1, pp. 152–66

Fisher, Stephen D. and Curtice, John, 'Tactical unwind? Changes in party preference structure and tactical voting in Britain between 2001 and 2005', *Journal of Elections, Public Opinion and Parties* (2006), vol. 16, no. 1, pp. 55–76

Foos, Florian and de Rooij, Eline, 'Household Partisan Composition and Voter Turnout: Investigating Experimental Spillover Effects between Cohabitants', paper presented at the 72nd Midwest Political Science Association Annual Conference, Chicago (2014)

Ford, Robert and Goodwin, Matthew, *Revolt on the Right: Explaining Support for the Radical Right in Britain* (London: Routledge, 2014)

Ford, Robert, Goodwin, Matthew J. and Cutts, David, 'Strategic Eurosceptics and Polite Xenophobes: Support for the United Kingdom Independence Party in the 2009 European Parliament elections', *European Journal of Political Research* (2012), vol. 51, no. 2, pp. 204–34

Franklin, Mark and Hobolt, Sara, 'The Legacy of Lethargy: How Elections to the European Parliament Depress Turnout', *Electoral Studies* (2011), vol. 30, no. 1, pp.67–76

Gerber, Alan S., Green, Donald P., and Larimer, Christopher W., 'Social Pressure and Voter Turnout: Evidence from a Large-scale Field Experiment', *American Political Science Review* (2008), vol. 102, no. 1, pp. 33–48

Gibson, Rachel and Cantijoch, Marta, 'Conceptualizing and Measuring Participation in the Age of the Internet: Is Online Political Engagement Really Different to Offline?', *The Journal of Politics* (2013), vol. 75, no. 3, pp. 701–716

Gorecki, Maciej and Marsh, Michael, 'Not just "friends and neighbours": canvassing, geographic proximity and voter choice', *European Journal of Political Research* (2012), vol. 51, no. 5, pp. 563–82

Heath, Anthony, Fisher, Stephen, Rosenblatt, Gemma, Sanders, David and Sobolewska, Maria, *The Political Integration of Ethnic Minorities in Britain* (Oxford: Oxford University Press, 2013)

Heath, Anthony; Jowell, Roger and Curtice, John, *The Rise of New Labour: Party Policies and Voter Choices* (Oxford: Oxford University Press, 2001)

Heath, Anthony, Jowell, Roger, Taylor, Bridget and Thomson, Katarina, 'Euroscepticism and the Referendum Party', *British Elections and Parties Yearbook*

(1998) vol. 8, pp. 95–110

Henderson, A., *Hierarchies of Belonging: National Identity and Political Culture in Scotland and Quebec* (Montreal-Kingston: McGill-Queen's University Press, 2007)

Henn, Matt and Foard, Nick, 'Young people, political participation and trust in Britain', *Parliamentary Affairs* (2012), vol. 65, no. 1, pp. 47–67

Hibbing, John R. and Marsh, David, 'Accounting for the Voting Patterns of British MPs on Free Votes', *Legislative Studies Quarterly* (1987), vol. 12, no. 2, pp. 275–97

Hibbing John R., Smith, Kevin B. and Alford, John R., *Predisposed* (London, Routledge, 2014)

Hobolt, Sara B., *Europe in Question: Referendums on European Integration* (Oxford: Oxford University Press, 2009)

Hudson, David and van Heerde-Hudson, Jennifer, 'A Mile Wide and an Inch Deep', *International Journal of Development Education and Global Learning* (2012), vol. 4, no. 1, pp. 5–23

Inglehart, Ronald, and Norris, Pippa, 'The developmental theory of the gender gap: women and men's voting behaviour in global perspective', *International Political Science Review* (2000), vol. 21, no. 4, pp. 441–62

Jennings, Will and Wlezien, Christopher, 'Distinguishing between Most Important Problems and Issues?', *Public Opinion Quarterly* (2011), vol. 75, no. 3, pp. 545–55

Johns, Robert and Shephard, Mark, 'Facing the Voters: The Potential Impact of Ballot Paper Photographs', *Political Studies* (2011), vol. 59, no. 3, pp. 636–58

Johnston, Ron, Pattie, Charles and Allsopp, J. G., *A Nation Dividing? The Electoral Map of Great Britain, 1979–1987* (London: Longmans, 1988)

Johnston, Ron, Pattie, Charles, Dorling, Danny and Rossiter, David, *From Votes to Seats: the Operation of the UK Electoral System since 1945* (Manchester:

Manchester University Press, 2001)

Johnston, Ron, Pattie, Charles and Rossiter, David, 'The election results in the UK regions' in Norris, Pippa and Wlezien, Christopher, (eds) *Britain Votes 2005* (Oxford: Oxford University Press, 2005), pp. 130–45

Johnston, Ron and Pattie, Charles, 'The British general election of 2010: a three-party contest or three two-party contests?', *The Geographical Journal* (2011), vol. 177, no. 1, pp. 17–26

Johnston, Ron, Cutts, David, Pattie, Charles and Fisher, Justin, 'We've got them on the list: contacting, canvassing and voting in a British general election campaigning', *Electoral Studies* (2012), vol. 31, no. 2, pp. 317–29

Johnston, Ron, Pattie, Charles, Cutts, David, Fieldhouse, Edward and Fisher, Justin, 'The Long and the Short of it: Local Campaigning at the British 2010 General Election', *Political Studies* (2013), vol. 61, pp. 114–37

Johnston, Ron and Pattie, Charles, *Money and Electoral Politics: Local Parties and Funding at General Elections* (Bristol: The Policy Press, 2014)

Johnston, Ron 'Which Map? Which Government? Malapportionment and Gerrymandering UK Style', *Government and Opposition*, Leonard Schapiro Memorial Lecture (2014), vol. 49, pp. 1–23

Kahneman, Daniel, *Thinking, Fast and Slow* (London: Allen Lane, 2011)

Kahr, Brett, *Sex and the Psyche: The Truth About Our Most Secret Fantasies* (London, Penguin, 2008)

Kellner, Peter 'Why Northerners Don't Vote Tory' [http://yougov.co.uk/news/2013/10/21/why-northerners-dont-vote-tory/], 21 October 2013

Kettlewell, Kelly and Phillips, Liz, *Census of Local Authority Councillors 2013* (Slough: LGA Research Report, May 2014)

Korris, Matt, *A Year in the Life: from member of public to Member of Parliament* (London: Hansard Society, 2011)

Langer, Ana Ines, *The Personalisation of Politics in the UK: Mediated Leadership from Attlee to Cameron* (Manchester: Manchester University Press, 2012)

Lawless, Jennifer and Fox, Richard, *It Takes a Candidate* (Cambridge: Cambridge University Press, 2005)

LeDuc, Lawrence, 'Referendums and Elections: How Do Campaigns Differ?', in Farrell, David M. and Schmitt-Beck, Rüdiger, (eds) *Do Political Campaigns Matter? Campaign Effects in Elections and Referendums* (London: Routledge, 2001), pp 145–62

Lee, Lucy and Young, Penny, 'A disengaged Britain? Political interest and participation over 30 years', in Park, Alison, Bryson, Caroline, Clery, Elizabeth, Curtice, John and Philips, Miranda, (eds) *British Social Attitudes 30* (London: NatCen, 2013)

Lerner, Jennifer S. and Keltner, Dacher, 'Fear, anger, and risk', *Journal of Personality and Social Psychology* (2001), vol. 81, no. 1, pp. 146–59

Lewis-Beck, Michael S., *Economics and Elections: the major Western democracies* (Ann Arbor, MI: Michigan University Press, 1988)

MacAllister, Ian, 'The dynamics of one-partyism', *Llafur* (1980), vol. 3, no. 2, pp. 79–89

Marcus, George E., Neuman, W. Russell and MacKuen, Michael B., *Affective intelligence and political judgment* (Chicago: The University of Chicago Press, 2000)

Marcus, George E., *Political psychology: Neuroscience, genetics, and politics* (Oxford: Oxford University Press, 2013)

Mattes, Kyle and Milazzo, Caitlin, 'Pretty Faces, Marginal Races: Predicting Election Outcomes using Positive and Negative Trait Assessments of British Parliamentary Candidate Images' *Electoral Studies* (2014), vol. 34, pp. 177–89

McGarry, John and O'Leary, Brendan, *The Northern Ireland Conflict: Consociational Engagements* (Oxford: Oxford University Press, 2004)

Milner, Helen and Tingley, Dustin 'Public Opinion and Foreign Aid', *International Interactions* (2013), vol. 39, no. 3, pp. 389–401

Modood, Tariq, *Multicultural Politics: Racism, ethnicity and Muslims in Britain* (Edinburgh: Edinburgh University Press, 2005)

Moon, Nick, *Opinion Polls: History, Theory and Practice* (Manchester: Manchester University Press, 1999)

Mudde, Cas, *Populist Radical Right Parties in Europe* (Cambridge: Cambridge University Press, 2007)

Myatt, David P. and Fisher, Stephen D., 'Tactical Coordination in Plurality Electoral Systems', *Oxford Review of Economic Policy* (2002), vol. 18, no. 4, pp. 504–522

Nickerson, David W., 'Is Voting Contagious? Evidence from Two Field Experiments', *American Political Science Review* (2008), vol. 102, no. 1, pp. 49–57

Norris, Pippa, 'Gender: a gender-generation gap?', in Evans, Geoffrey and Norris, Pippa, (eds) *Critical Elections: British Parties and Voters in Long-Term Perspective* (London: Sage, 1999), pp. 146–63

— —, 'May's Law of Curvilinear Disparity Revisited: Leaders, Officers, Members and Voters in British Political Parties', *Party Politics* (1995), vol. 1, no. 1, pp. 29–47

Olson, Ingrid R. and Marshuetz, Christy, 'Facial Attractiveness is Appraised in a Glance', *Emotion* (2005), vol. 5, no. 4, pp. 498–502

Panagopolous, Costas, Larimer, Christopher W. and Condon, Meghan, 'Social Pressure, Descriptive Norms, and Voter Mobilization', *Political Behavior* (2014), vol. 36, no. 2, pp. 451–69

Park, David K., Gelman, Andrew and Bafumi, Joseph, 'Bayesian multilevel estimation with poststratification: state-level estimates from national polls', *Political Analysis* (2004), vol. 12, no. 4, pp. 375–85

Payne, Clive, 'Election forecasting in the UK: The BBC's experience', *EurAmerica* (2003), vol. 33, no. 1, pp. 193–234

Phillips, Anne, *The Politics of Presence* (Oxford, Oxford University Press, 1995)

Philpot, Tasha and Walton, Hanes, 'One of Our Own: Black Female Candidates and the Voters Who Support Them', *American Journal of Political Science*

(2007), vol. 51, no. 1, pp. 49–62

Procedure Committee of the House of Commons, *Sitting hours and the Parliamentary calendar* (London: HMSO, 2012)

Puig-i-Abril, Eulalia and Rojas, Hernando, 'Being Early on the Curve: Online Practices and Expressive Political Participation', *International Journal of Internet Science* (2007), vol. 2, no. 1, pp. 28–44

— —, 'Mobilizers Mobilized: Information, Expression, Mobilization and Participation in the Digital Age', *Journal of Computer-Mediated Communication* (2009), vol. 14, no. 4, pp. 902–927

Puwar, Nirmal, *Space Invaders: Race, Gender and Bodies Out of Place* (Oxford, Bloomsbury Academic, 2004)

Rallings, Colin and Thrasher, Michael, *Local Elections in Britain* (London: Routledge, 1997)

— —, 'Another (small) step on the road towards a multi-party Britain: turnout and party choice at the 2009 local and European Parliament elections', *British Politics* (2009), vol. 4, pp. 463–77

Rallings, Colin, Thrasher, Michael and Borisyuk, Galina, 'Unused votes in English Local Government Elections: Effects and Explanations', *Journal of Elections, Public Opinion and Parties* (2009), vol. 19, no. 1, pp. 1–23

Rallings, Colin, Thrasher, Michael, Borisyuk, Galina and Shears, Mary, *The 2009 Survey of Local Election Candidates* (London: Improvement and Development Agency, 2009)

— —, 'Parties, recruitment and modernisation: Evidence from local election candidates', *Local Government Studies* (2010), vol. 36, no. 3, pp. 361–79

Saggar, Shamit, *Race and Representation: Electoral politics and ethnic pluralism in Britain* (Manchester: Manchester University Press, 2000)

Sanbonmatsu, Kira, 'Gender-Related Political Knowledge and the Descriptive Representation of Women', *Political Behavior* (2003), vol. 25, no. 4, pp. 367–88

Sanders, David, 'Government Popularity and the Next General Election', *Political*

Quarterly (1991), vol. 62, no. 2, pp. 235–61

——, 'The dynamics of party identification', in Clarke, Harold, Sanders, David, Stewart, Marianne and Whiteley, Paul, *Political Choice in Britain* (Oxford: Oxford University Press, 2004)

——, 'Popularity Function Forecasts for the 2005 UK General Election', *British Journal of Politics and International Relations* (2005), vol. 7, no. 2, pp. 174–90

Schuman, Howard and Presser, Stanley, 'Public Opinion and Public Ignorance: The Fine Line between Attitude and Nonattitude', *American Journal of Sociology* (1980), vol. 85, no. 5, pp. 1214–25

Schuman, Howard and Presser, Stanley, *Questions and Answers in Attitude Surveys*, reprint edn (London, Sage, 1996)

Seyd, Patrick and Whiteley, Paul, *Labour's Grassroots* (Oxford: Clarendon Press, 1992)

——, *New Labour's Grassroots* (Basingstoke: Palgrave, 2002)

Sobolewska, Maria, 'Party strategies, political opportunity structure and the descriptive representation of ethnic minorities in Britain', *West European Politics* (2013), vol. 36, no. 3, pp. 615–33

Special issue of *Electoral Studies* 'Consequences of low turnout', Lutz, Georg and Marsh, Michael, (eds) (2007), vol. 26, no. 3

Special issue of *Electoral Studies* 'The UK Electoral System Referendum, May 2011', Laycock, Samantha, Renwick, Alan, Stevens, Daniel and Vowles, Jack, (eds) (2013), vol. 32, no. 2

Special issue of *Information, Communication & Society* 'The Networked Young Citizen', Loader, Brian D., Vromen, Ariadne and Xenos, Michael A., (eds) (2014), vol. 17, no. 2

Stevens, Daniel, Banducci, Susan, Karp, Jeffrey and Vowles, Jack, 'Priming Time for Blair? Media Priming, Iraq, and Leadership Evaluations in Britain', *Electoral Studies* (2011), vol. 30, no. 3, pp. 546–60

Stevens, Daniel and Karp, Jeffrey, 'Leadership Traits and Media Influence in Britain', *Political Studies* (2012), vol. 60, no. 4, pp. 787–808

Sturgis, Patrick and Smith, Patten, 'Fictitious Issues Revisited: Political Interest,

Knowledge and the Generation of Nonattitudes', *Political Studies* (2010), vol. 58, no. 1, pp. 66–84

Tesler, Michael, 'The Spillover of Racialization into Evaluations of Bo Obama' [http://today.yougov.com/news/2012/04/10/spillover-racialization-evalua-tions-bo-obama/] (2012)

— —, 'The Spillover of Racialization into Health Care: How President Obama Polarized Public Opinion by Racial Attitudes and Race', *American Journal of Political Science* (2012), vol. 56, no. 6, pp. 690–704

Tesler, Michael and Sears, David, *Obama's Race: The 2008 Election and the Dream of a Post-Racial America* (Chicago: University of Chicago Press, 2010)

The Electoral Commission, *Age of Electoral Majority Report* (The Electoral Commission, 2004)

The Youth Citizenship Commission, *Making the Connection* (The Youth Citizenship Commission, 2007)

Thrasher, Michael, Borisyuk, Galina, Rallings, Colin and Shears, Mary, 'BAME Candidates in Local Elections in Britain', *Parliamentary Affairs* (2013), vol. 66, no. 2, pp. 286–304

Thrasher, Michael, Borisyuk, Galina, Rallings, Colin, and Webber, Richard, 'Candidate Ethnic Origins and Voter Preferences: Examining Voting Bias in Local Elections in Britain' paper presented at the 71st Midwest Political Science Association Annual Conference, Chicago (2013)

Tilley, James and Hobolt, Sara, 'Is the Government to Blame? An Experimental Test of How Partisanship Shapes Perceptions of Performance and Responsibility', *Journal of Politics* (2011), vol. 73, no. 2, pp. 316–30

Todorov, Alexander, Mandisodza, Anesu N., Goren, Amir and Hall, Crystal C., 'Inferences of Competence from Faces Predict Election Outcomes', *Science* (2005), vol. 308, no. 5728, pp. 1623–26

Van der Eijk, Cees, Schmitt, Hermann and Sapir, Eliyahu, 'The Electoral Consequences of Low Turnout in European Parliament Elections', in Rosema,

Martin, Denters, Bas and Aarts, Kees, (eds) *How Democracy Works* (Pallas – Amsterdam University Press, 2011), pp. 183-198

Van der Eijk, Cees, and Van Egmond, Marcel, 'Political effects of low turnout in national and European elections', *Electoral Studies* (2007), 26, pp.561–73

Van Heerde-Hudson, Jennifer and Fisher, Justin, 'Parties heed (with caution): Public knowledge of and attitudes towards party finance in Britain', *Party Politics* (2013), vol. 19, no. 1, pp. 41–60

Vivyan, Nick and Wagner, Markus, 'House or Home: Constituent preferences over the activities of representatives', *Working Paper*, Durham University (2014)

Wagner, Markus, 'Fear and anger in Great Britain: blame assignment and emotional reactions to the financial crisis', *Political Behavior* (2014), vol. 36, no. 3, pp. 683–703

Wagner, Markus, Johann, David and Kritzinger, Sylvia, 'Voting at 16: Turnout and the quality of vote choice', *Electoral Studies* (2012), vol. 31, no. 2, pp. 372–83

Webber, Richard, Rallings, Colin, Borisyuk, Galina, and Thrasher, Michael, 'Ballot Order Positional Effects in British Local Elections, 1973–2011', *Parliamentary Affairs* (2013), vol. 67, no. 1, pp. 119–36

Wilson, Glenn D., 'Ideology and Humor Preferences', *International Political Science Review* (1990), vol. 11, no. 4, pp. 461–72

— —, 'Conservatism and Art Preferences', *Journal of Personality and Social Psychology* (1973), vol. 25, no. 2, pp. 286–88

Whiteley, Paul, 'Where have all the Members Gone?', *Parliamentary Affairs* (2009), vol. 62, no. 2, pp. 242–57

Whiteley, Paul, Clarke, Harold, Sanders, David and Stewart, Marianne, *Affluence, Austerity and Electoral Change in Britain* (Cambridge: Cambridge University Press, 2013)

Whiteley, Paul, Seyd, Patrick and Billinghurst, Antony, *Third Force Politics* (Oxford: Oxford University Press, 2006)

Whiteley, Paul, Seyd, Patrick and Richardson, Jeremy, *True Blues* (Oxford:

Oxford University Press, 1994)

Winters, Kristi and Campbell, Rosie, 'Hearts or Minds: Men, Women and Leader Evaluations in the 2005 General Election', in Wring, Dominic, Green, Jane, Mortimore, Roger and Atkinson, Simon, (eds) *Political Communications: The General Election Campaign of 2005* (Basingstoke: Palgrave Macmillan, 2007), pp. 184–202

Winters, Kristi and Carvalho, Edzia, '2010 British General Election Leader Evaluations: Replicating Electoral Focus Group Research', *The Qualitative Report* (2013), vol. 18, article 88, pp. 1–21

Wlezien, Christopher, 'The Public as Thermostat: dynamics of preferences for spending', *American Journal of Political Science* (1995), vol. 39, no. 4, pp. 981–1000

Wyn Jones, Richard, Scully, Roger and Trystan, Dafydd, 'Why do the Conservatives always do (even) worse in Wales?', *British Elections and Parties Review* (2002), vol. 12, no. 1, pp. 229–45

Wyn Jones, R., Lodge, Guy, Henderson, Ailsa and Wincott, Daniel, *The Dog That Finally Barked* (London: Institute for Public Policy Research, 2012)

Wyn Jones, R. and Scully, R., *Wales Says Yes* (Cardiff: University of Wales Press, 2012)

Wyn Jones, R., Lodge, Guy, Jeffery, Charlie, Gottfried, Glen, Scully, Roger, Henderson, Ailsa and Wincott, Daniel, *England and its Two Unions* (London: Institute for Public Policy Research, 2013)

Zogby, John, *The Way We'll Be* (London: Random House, 2009)

Zuckerman, Alan, Dasovic, Josip and Fitzgerald, Jennifer, *Partisan Families: The Social Logic of Bounded Partisanship in Germany and Britain* (Cambridge: Cambridge University Press, 2007)

Index

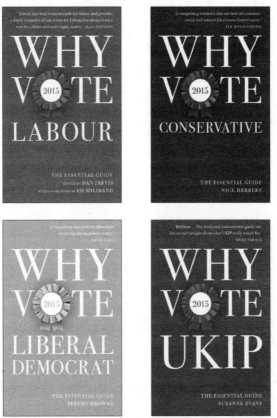

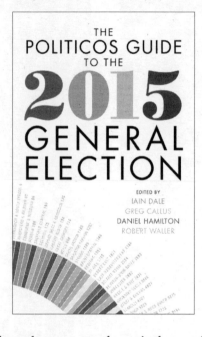